DIVING AND SNORKELING GUID

Australia

Southeast Coast and Tasmania

Peter Stone

Pisces Books
A division of Gulf Publishing Company
Houston, Texas

Publisher's note: At the time of publication of this book, all the information was determined to be as accurate as possible. However, when you use this guide, new construction may have changed land reference points, weather may have altered reef configurations, and some businesses may no longer be in operation. Your assistance in keeping future editions up-to-date will be greatly appreciated.

Also, please pay particular attention to the diver rating system in this book. Know your limits!

Pisces Books
A division of Gulf Publishing Company
P.O. Box 2608, Houston, Texas 77252-2608

Library of Congress Cataloging-in-Publication Data

Stone, Peter.
    Diving and snorkeling guide to Australia: southeast coast and Tasmania / Peter Stone.
        p.   cm.
    Includes index.
    ISBN 1-55992-059-9
    1. Skin diving—Australia—Guide-books. 2. Scuba diving—Australia—Guide-books. 3. Australia—Description and Travel—1981—Guide-books. I. Title.
GV840.S78S825   1992
797.2'3—dc20   91-39840
                                                                      CIP

Printed in Hong Kong

10 9 8 7 6 5 4 3 2 1

Table of Contents

Acknowledgments

The author appreciates the assistance provided by several experienced divers and dive operators who have verified the text and provided photographs: Bill Antico (Byron Bay Dive), Ross Clifford (Sundive, Byron Bay), Andy and Elena Ireland (Coffs Harbour Dive), Noel Hitchins (South West Rocks Dive), Denis Kemp (Action Divers Tuncurry), Glen Percy (Aqua Sports, Sydney), Sue Sainsbury (Shiprock Dive, Sydney), Adrian Cookson (Jervis Bay Sea Sports), Darryl Stuart (Darryl's Tackle and Dive, Narooma), Paul and Elaine Cozens (Sea Trek, Tathra), Dave Warth (Merimbula), Tony Douglas (Byron Bay), Peter Ronald (Flagstaff Hill Maritime Village), Chris and Cathy Deane (Adelaide). Several divers have kindly supplied photographs (acknowledged with captions).

The Historic Shipwreck Act 1976 has virtually put an end to looting of the thousands of ships that have gone down since settlement. Although no caches of gold sovereigns are to be found off the southeast coast, divers find treasure in other less valuable items.

How to Use This Guide

This guide does not attempt to cover all the superb dive sites over the 5,000 or so miles of Australia's southeastern coastline; to do so would require many substantial volumes. In order to be informative and yet concise, the most popular dive *regions* have been identified. There may well be many dive sites within each region, but once again, only the most popular sites have been identified, to give an overview of the attractions of each region. Visiting divers will be guided by local dive operators to the better sites according to their dive charter schedules.

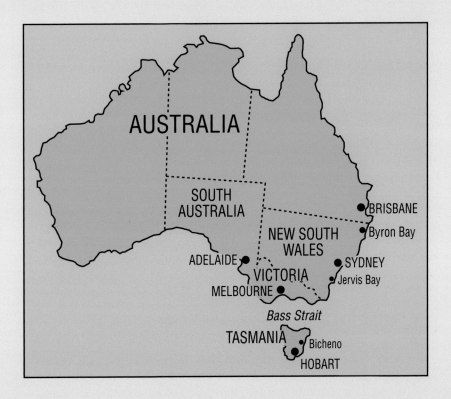

Because of the diversity of sites, the headings commencing each region are by necessity only a general indication. Most regions have shallow water diving and snorkelling, even if it is not listed as one of the main sites. Divers must *always* be aware of local current, weather, and sea conditions, hence specific cautions have not been included throughout the book. It is important to remember that all open ocean diving is subjected to tide and current, waves, and surge to varying degrees and that safety demands obtaining local knowledge before entering the sea.

It is stressed that visiting divers entering unfamiliar waters should, preferably, dive with a recognized dive charter operator. Not only is this a safety consideration, but it is in the interests of local operators to take divers to the best sites. Once you have become familiar with an area, then by all means "do your own thing," but always obtain up-to-date information on the weather, prevailing sea conditions, and shipping movements, if relevant. This is standard procedure for diving anywhere.

Although this book is a guide to diving, Australia has many wonderful attractions topside. The coastline from Byron Bay on the central east coast clockwise to Ceduna on the central south coast includes diverse landscape, cities and towns, people, flora, and fauna. From dense natural bush and forest to miles of rolling sand dunes, from sheep and cattle grazing hills to picturesque rows of grape vines, from precipitous cliffs to long surf beaches, southeast Australia has it all. Included in the scope of this book are four capital cities, all offering their own unique contribution to the Australian lifestyle.

The aim of this guide is to give the unfamiliar visitor an opportunity to determine beforehand just what it is that each region has to offer — in terms of diving, topside interest, facilities, and charter services. It does not aim to be a definitive guide — that can only be your own logbook.

The Rating System for Divers and Dives

Because there are many different sites in each region, the expertise rating indicated for the region is at best general and conservative.

A *Novice* is a recently qualified diver or a more generally experienced diver who has not dived for some time or is not familiar with the specific diving conditions of the region. An *Intermediate* diver is one who has been actively diving for at least a year and is familiar with the general

The southern blue-ringed octopus (Hapalochlaena maculosa) *displays distinctive pulsating blue rings when in an aggressive state. The tiny creature is less than six inches across, yet packs a deadly venom. It is definitely not to be handled. Photo courtesy of Adrian Neuman.*

conditions of the dive. An *Experienced* diver is one who has been diving regularly for many years and is familiar with the conditions of the region. An *Advanced* diver has specific advanced diving qualifications such as wreck diving, deep diving, or cave diving and is familiar with the conditions of the particular dive. Needless to say, all divers should be physically fit and mentally attuned to diving. Whereas it is appreciated that experienced and advanced divers can competently dive novice and intermediate sites, it is recognized that they would usually prefer dives more relevant to their experience.

Australian dive charter operators will insist on seeing a relevant qualification card. It is also advisable to have a logbook of recent dives. It is foolish to attempt a dive beyond your capabilities. If it appears that a good dive is beyond your experience, most dive operators will arrange for a "hand-hold" supervisory dive with an instructor or advanced diver. A lack of experience will generally not preclude the diver from a good dive site, providing the charter operator is informed accordingly. PADI, NAUI, SSI, NASDS, FAUI, BSAC are all recognized.

1

Southeast Australia — An Overview

Australia is an island continent roughly the same size as the U.S.A. The continent has three main physiographic regions — the Western Plateau, the Central Lowlands, and the Eastern Highlands, also known as the Great Dividing Range. The greater proportion of the central-western inland area is dry, with desert sand plateaus and low bush scrub. The Aussies call it the "outback." A fertile coastal plain separates the eastern mountains from the sea and the majority of Australians live here along the Pacific coast. The greatest population concentration is in the industrial and commercial belt between Newcastle and Woollongong, encompassing Sydney, the largest city.

Australia is divided into six states: New South Wales, Victoria, South Australia, Tasmania, Queensland, Western Australia; and the Northern Territory. Each has a capital, respectively Sydney, Melbourne, Adelaide, Hobart, Brisbane, Perth, and Darwin. In addition, there is the Australian capital, Canberra, located inland within the Australian Capital Territory. This guide covers the New South Wales coastal plain, south to Victoria's rich Gippsland rural area, and west toward and beyond Adelaide. And, of course, the beautiful island of Tasmania is included too.

Visitors to Australia are often intimidated by the vast distances between towns, but this is not so predominant in the southeast. There is an excellent road system along the coastal fringe with commercial centers, fishing villages, and holiday resorts separated by no more than fifty miles at most. Australia may have its remote "outback" but visitors need not be concerned about being stranded in the southeast.

The majority of the southeast region is defined as "warm temperate, rainy with no dry season, and hot summers." The northern New South Wales coast has weather as perfect as anywhere in the world. December to February are the summer months.

Entry into Australia is usually through Sydney or Melbourne, although all the capital cities have international airports. A vast domestic air network links all major cities and rural centers. Comfortable railways join the capital cities, while coach services link all major cities, and rural and coastal towns.

A variety of dive boats are used along the southeastern coast of Australia. Larger boats like the converted ketch Falie *seen here in the Great Australian Bight transfer divers to sites in inflatable boats or small runabouts — "rubber ducks" or "tinnies."*

Remote and rugged Green Cape in the Ben Boyd National Park juts into the Tasman Sea south of Eden, one of the finest shore dive regions in Australia.

Perhaps the best way to see Australia and enjoy a variety of diving is to hire a car at your international arrival point and drive along the coast. Cars may be dropped off at other major centers so that a return journey may be made by air, rail, or coach. There is no shortage of motels along the coastal stretches, but it is usually necessary to pre-book if travelling during school holidays. Australians drive on the left side of the road.

Despite Australia's multiculturalism, the national language is English (although some may find it difficult to understand the Aussie accent). In addition, there are many additional "Australian" words and different meanings to existing words. Australians rarely wrestle with crocodiles in outback pubs but the language used in *Crocodile Dundee* was fair dinkum.

Your travel agent will no doubt acquaint you with other idiosyncracies of Australian life. Sufficient to say that you will certainly need a passport to enter and exit the country, and in some instances a temporary visitor's visa may be required. Tipping is customary in taxis, hotels, and restaurants. Electric power is 3-pin 240-volt, however, most international hotels and some dive charter boats have 110-volt systems also.

2

Diving In Southeast Australia

With more than 20,000 miles of magnificent coastline and 80% of the population living in close proximity to the sea, it is little wonder that Australians enjoy scuba diving and all forms of water sport. Dive sites are rarely crowded, and good dive charter facilities exist in most popular regions.

Overseas divers tend to think of the Great Barrier Reef when discussing diving in Australia. Yet Australia offers some of the finest temperate water diving in the world. Diving the southeastern states will pose no problem to the diver who is interested enough to travel and see what Australia has to offer. The visitor has the option of being free to drive

Rich and varied marine life covers most protected reefs and walls throughout the temperate waters of southeastern Australia.

along the coast seeking good diving sites, or may join an organized trip from one of the many dive shops in the capital cities or coastal towns.

Each Australian state has something different to offer; open ocean reefs and tiny islands, protected bays, wrecks, prolific marine life, and freshwater caves.

Certification

Dive shops and dive charter operators will require the diver to be certified to a recognized standard. Australian divers are trained to one of four major scuba diving standards: National Association of Scuba Diving Schools–Australia (NASDS) incorporating the standards and procedures of the Federation of Australian Underwater Instructors (FAUI), the Professional Association of Diving Instructors (PADI), the National Association of Underwater Instructors (NAUI), and more recently, Scuba Schools International (SSI). Overseas visitors may well be qualified to other standards; most are recognized.

Dive courses are available in all capital cities and in many coastal and inland towns and islands. Courses may be taken over evenings and weekends spanning several weeks, or over an intensive five days. The training is thorough, yet paced to suit the student. Australia has a high standard of diving instruction with a commensurate standard of diver.

Not all dive schools are as well equipped as John Griffiths' Scuba Centre in Wynyard on Tasmania's north coast, but all have access to training pools and the latest equipment.

The magpie perch (Cheilodactylus nigripes), *recognized by its two, wide, dark brown body bands, is common on exposed and protected reefs off Australia's south coast, often sheltering under jetties and within rock formations.*

Dive Services

All capital cities and major towns, and most coastal holiday resorts have at least one dive operator equipped with a registered dive charter boat, gear sales and hire, training facilities, and an airfill station. Not all, however, operate seven days a week. The weekends and school

There is a marked difference between tropical water diving and temperate water diving. Novice divers trained in tropical waters often find temperate water conditions demanding, to say the least, as they may not have experienced currents, cloudy water, rough seas, and thick wet suits. Many experienced tropical water divers must regard themselves as novices if they are inexperienced in temperate conditions. It is imperative that the diver appreciates the various conditions that he or she may not be confident with, and inform the charter operator accordingly. See page 90 for guidelines for diving in temperate water.

Comfortable dive lodges may be found in major dive centers, providing a complete package of accommodation, transport, and diving. Dive instruction is also available. This lodge is in Blairgowrie on Port Phillip Bay.

holidays are busy times. It is unwise to turn up at the dive store and expect to be booked on to the next dive. Always phone at least several days in advance to ensure boat space, and confirm this on the day of departure as weather conditions may result in the cancellation of a trip. Arrive in plenty of time to kit up, particularly if gear hire is required.

Some dive centers in popular regions have lodge accommodation and operate seven days a week. The standard of each dive operation varies but most have good facilities and are well organized. Dive boats tend to be of a design suitable for the region. For inshore diving near to base, inflatable boats are sometimes used, but generally all diving is from 20-ft-plus aluminum mono or twin hull boats purposely built for diving. Only a few dive operators have live-aboard boats, as most diving is within a day's trip of base.

Most city dive shops have regular weekend and day trips, and also holidays of several days' duration to distant sites. All services, including transport, are provided. See page 85 for a listing of dive services and organizations.

Accommodations

If joining an organized trip, accommodation will be provided, usually in a diver's lodge, camping, or in motels. Well equipped lodges exist in popular dive regions such as Byron Bay, Forster, Jervis Bay, Merimbula, Victoria's Mornington Peninsula, and Bicheno in Tasmania. The nomadic tourist with no specific itinerary can also stay in the dive lodges, but should book in advance, if possible. Motels and hotels are found in all coastal towns and are rarely fully booked. Australians have a reputation for hospitality, so you should never be caught without a bed for the night.

The Law

It is only since 1976 that Australia recognized the importance of protecting historic shipwrecks. The Commonwealth Historic Shipwreck Act is complemented by individual State Acts that encourage with rewards the reporting of new shipwrecks, and deter looting and destruction through heavy fines. The important rule to remember now is "look, but don't touch." Some historically sensitive wrecks are totally out-of-bounds.

Strict laws apply to the taking of marine animals for food, research, or display. These are defined and administered by state government Fisheries divisions and differ for each state. Check with local dive

Only a keen eye will observe the delicate brittle stars (Ophiotrichidae sp.) entwined on a sponge growing with a gorgonia sea fan.

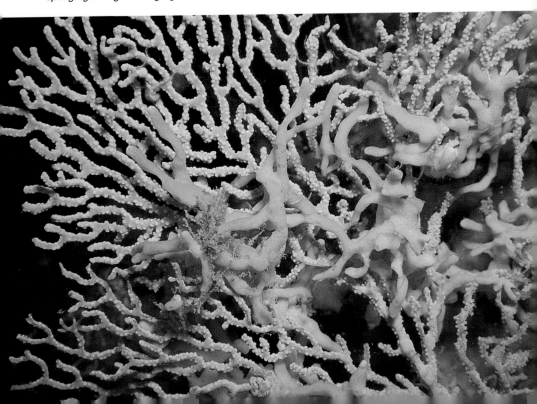

operators or the appropriate authorities before taking anything from the sea or inland waters.

All states have designated Marine Park Acts which provide laws to declare and administer specific coastlines and inland waters. Various conditions apply, but generally scuba diving in marine parks is allowed, but the taking of any marine life is prohibited.

Local councils and harbor trusts also have specific by-laws prohibiting scuba diving entry from jetties, although there is no legislation preventing scuba diving under a jetty if access is from boat or shore, and that no boat is hindered in the use of the pier. Likewise, specific laws apply to anchoring of boats in shipping channels.

Diver's Flag

Australia has adopted the Assembly of Intergovernmental Maritime Consultative Organization's code for International Code of Signals, and therefore recognizes International Code Flag "A" as being the "diver down" flag. This is a *blue and white* swallowtail flag and is interpreted to mean that a diver is below water and that boats must proceed at a slow speed and keep a lookout until clear of the area.

Conditions

The East Australian Current flows southward along the east coast at up to 1.5 knots, bringing warmer waters from the north and the Great Barrier Reef. This accounts for the prolific marine life off the northern New South Wales coast, where both temperate and tropical species may

The eastern side of Wilsons Promontory contains several superb coves, allowing shelter for yachts and dive boats.

be found. The current becomes broader and weaker as it reaches Sydney, but the momentum of flow results in counterclockwise eddies extending toward Tasmania. Currents play a significant role in the climate of the southeast and influence coastal and pelagic marine life.

Seasonal climates are traditional — hot in summer, mild to cold in winter. Cyclones (hurricanes) do not venture south into the regions covered by this book. Destructive storms can occur throughout the southeast mainland and Tasmania, but they are rare. Generally, the weather is sunny; winds range from calm to gusty, and a rainy overcast day is about the worst condition encountered while diving. Australia has a competent coastal weather reporting system, hence poor diving conditions are generally avoided.

Diving is available year-round, however seasonal changes occur. The best visibility tends to be in autumn and winter (March to August). These are also the most predictable seasons. Seas are calm even though some days may be overcast. From September through to January seas can come up at short notice so greater care is needed if venturing far offshore.

Holidays

Employed Australians have a minimum of four weeks leave a year and make every opportunity to travel and be outdoors. The main holiday period is from a few days before Christmas to the start of the school year in late January. Beach and holiday resorts are particularly crowded during the first two weeks of January. Easter also tends to be an active time. The school year is divided into four terms (semesters), with two weeks of holiday in between. Although resorts and motels are rarely booked up, it is wise to prebook.

And then there are the many long weekends and other single day holidays — the Queen's Birthday, the birth of Australia, Anzac Day (for veterans), Labour Day, and Melbourne Cup Day (a horse race).

Booking Arrangements

It is usual to prebook dive boat charters in conjunction with flights and other accommodation but this is more applicable to the Great Barrier Reef and does not generally apply to diving in the southeast. One great advantage of diving this region is the range of diving available, and hence mobility and flexibility should be objectives.

Dive holiday arrangements will depend on time available and starting point. For example, if time is limited and you are in Sydney, consider Jervis Bay; book directly or with a Sydney dive shop having a Jervis Bay trip — phone around. General travel agents will not be able to assist with dive bookings, but can, of course, arrange all transport and standard accommodation. If diver lodge accommodation is offered, contact the lodge directly or through an affiliated dive shop. Specialist dive travel agents in Australia should be able to assist with all booking arrangements, including diving. International dive travel agents prefer to book their own diver packages, but should be able to arrange all flights and accommodation, and provide advice complementing that contained in this guide. Remember, however, that most international dive travel agents are not familiar with diving southeast Australia. You really do need to do your own research and make dive bookings locally.

▶

Divers gear up in preparation for one of the finest dives off the southern Australia coast as the converted trading ketch Falie *approaches Topgallant Island in the Great Australian Bight.*

3

New South Wales Coast

Byron Bay

Typical depth range:	Many sites; 10-140 feet
Typical current conditions:	None within bay, slight to moderate in open ocean
Expertise required:	Novice to experienced; good training region
Access:	Boat and shore

Byron Bay is the easternmost point of Australia, and consequently the closest to the Pacific Ocean continental shelf; it is 55 miles south of Coolangatta on Queensland's Gold Coast, and 500 miles north of Sydney.

The Cape Byron lighthouse stands on a rocky promontory overlooking Byron Bay, the most easterly point on the Australian mainland.

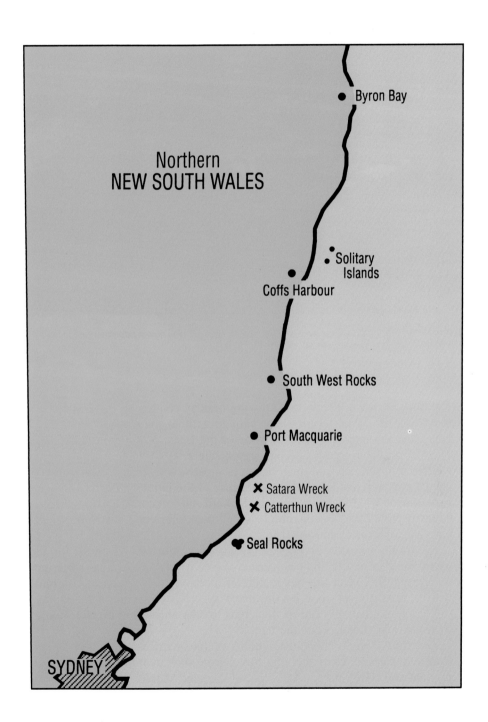

Northern
NEW SOUTH WALES

● Byron Bay

●
● Solitary
  Islands
● Coffs Harbour

● South West Rocks

● Port Macquarie

✖ Satara Wreck
✖ Catterthun Wreck

♥ Seal Rocks

SYDNEY

Solitary Islands — Coffs Harbour

Typical depth range:	30-80 feet
Typical current conditions:	Moderate
Expertise required:	Intermediate to Experienced
Access:	Boat

Coffs Harbour, 350 miles north of Sydney and 200 miles south of Brisbane on the Pacific Highway, is a prime tourist region with excellent surfing beaches, rain forests, banana plantations, flora and fauna reserves, fishing, boating, and many other holiday attractions. It also offers some of the finest diving on the east coast with the nearby Solitary Islands providing an abundance of temperate and tropical fish, sponges, and coral.

The red morwong (Cheildactylus fuscus) *frequents reefs along the central east coast of Australia, often in schools of more than a hundred.*

The Solitary Islands lie where warmer waters from the north and the colder southern seas entwine. Both tropical and temperate species can be found off the mainland shore and throughout the islands. Marine life is varied, colorful, and prolific. Great schools of kingfish, mackerel, and giant Queensland grouper are regularly seen. There are extensive areas of hard coral formations. Manta rays are frequently seen on their annual pilgrimage to North West Solitary Island from December to June, whilst whales can be seen from June to November.

The Solitary Islands can be reached only by boat, and those islands furthest out have the clearest water. Mullaway, a tiny coastal village just 25 miles north of Coffs Harbour, is the best departure point for the North Solitary Islands, and North West Solitary Island can best be reached from Red Rock. North Solitary Island consists of two larger islands and one small islet, about 9 miles offshore from Mullaway, 20 miles north of Coffs Harbour.

The *South Solitary Islands* lie 3 miles offshore, about 6 miles northeast of Coffs Harbour, and consist of five scattered islands and a number of pinnacles and reefs. The two groups are separated by about 15 miles. In addition there are several other islands, rocks, and reefs in the area, including Split Solitary Island halfway between Coffs Harbour and South Solitary Island.

The northern end of *South Solitary Island* extends down in a series of deep crevices and overhangs: ideal hiding places for Wobbegong sharks, turtles and fish. Beyond the crevices are large weather-worn boulders broken away from the island. The bottom slopes away to around 85 ft. Fish life abounds with grouper, parrotfish, flutemouths, morwongs, lionfish, and occasional visits by large pelagics such as kingfish and Spanish mackerel.

Separated from South Solitary by a narrow channel, *The Arch* is a majestic rock formation whose sheer walls extend underwater. Several large gutters lead towards deep cuts in the rock, caves, or to the Arch itself. The underwater terrain makes this a beautiful dive.

Northern Coast, New South Wales

Typical depth range:	30-80 feet, with two deep wrecks
Typical current conditions:	Can be rough
Expertise required:	Intermediate to advanced
Access:	Boat and shore; snorkelling along the coast

On the drive north from Sydney along the Pacific Highway a sign every so often will point to a quiet village on the coast or perhaps one of the many lakes just inland. The coastline is interesting even for the non-diver with high rocky headlands bordering long white beaches, river entrances feeding huge lakes, and offshore reefs and islands hugging the coast and stretching for miles in either direction. This area is known for its beauty and superb climate. The diving is excellent with schooling kingfish and Spanish mackerel and interesting terrain. The region is known for its magnificent nudibranchs and brightly colored tube worms.

The major town, Port Macquarie, lies on the Hastings River about halfway between Sydney and the Queensland border. Typical of the diving is *Lighthouse Reef*, covered in sponges and gorgonia, and with prolific fish life. The *Pinnacles* rise from about 100 ft to within 30 ft of the surface and are riddled with small caves and crevices. The walls are covered in sponges, gorgonia, hydroids, and sea tulips, and are teeming with fish.

The quiet coastal village of South West Rocks, on Trial Bay 50 miles north of Port Macquarie, is well-known for just one of its several dive sites. *Fish Rock*, just one mile south of Smoky Cape, is one of the finest dives off the northern New South Wales coast. The magnificent and varied underwater terrain includes a long swim-through tunnel, drop-offs, ridges, and caves. Fish life is abundant and the sponge gardens are magnificent. *Fish Rock Cave* is an exciting dive with a challenging 300 ft swim-through. The shallow end of the cave is in 30 ft of water and extends down to about 80 ft. Hard and soft corals, gorgonia fans, Wobbegong sharks, and crayfish abound.

Grey nurse sharks lie motionless at *Shark Gutters* at the southern end of Fish Rock, three huge gutters which peak at 60 ft. *Black Rock,* southwest of Fish Rock, is also an excellent dive. Plate coral is predominant and fish life prolific; this is an excellent shallow dive, especially for the novice diver.

Holiday towns Forster and Tuncurry lie on Wallis Lake 210 miles north of Sydney and have all facilities. *Latitude Rock* is an outcrop with four excellent dive sites: the *Inner Reef*, the *Amphitheatre, Cod Holes,* and the *Sponge Gardens*. Fish life is prolific and friendly: large tame blue

The spotted wobbegong (Orectolobus maculatus) *and his cousin, the banded wobbegong, can be aggressive if molested. Generally, however, they lie peacefully on the seabed, seemingly unconcerned by flashing strobes and inquisitive divers. Wobbegongs are common in southern waters, the spotted wobbegong particularly so off the central eastern coast.*

groupers, masses of moray eels, turtles, and Wobbegong and grey nurse sharks.

Boulder Reef is a large rambling reef off Blackhead Beach with many crevices frequently visited by grey nurse sharks. Depth range is 20 to 50 feet. The site is known for its proliferation of nudibranchs — up to twenty different species can be found here. A large cavern in the cliff face near the lighthouse called the *Thunderhole* opens to the surface with an air chamber and blowhole usually only diveable in calm seas. Schools of large jewfish have been seen inside and large bullrays on the seabed at 35 ft.

A thousand species of minute animals may live in just one square yard of reef ledge in temperate waters. Bright purple ascidians are surrounded by sponges and algae.

Bird Island, one of the best dives in the Forster area, lies just off Boat Beach and can be dived from shore or boat. Relatively shallow, the island is surrounded with teeming fish life including turtles and grey nurse sharks.

Other excellent sites in the region include *Graveyard Reef* and *Skeleton Reef* with deep drop-offs and prolific marine life, particularly schooling red morwong.

Seal Rocks village, 22 miles south of Forster, is only a sleepy hollow with a lonely general store, but it is the launching place for some great diving. *Seal Rocks,* comprising Big Seal (about 500 yards long), Little Seal, and submerged Little Seal Bommie are about a mile and a half in front of the lighthouse. Pelagic fish must regard this as their meeting place, particularly sharks and kingfish. The rocky underwater terrain of pinnacles, gutters, caves, swim-throughs, and drop-offs are covered in sponge gardens and all manner of marine life. Divers can move among blackfish, large stingrays, and blue groupers, and during the summer months, yellowtail kingfish, mackerel, tuna, and deepsea mullet are attracted by the large schools of pilchards and tiny bait fish. Sharks are also usually found around the Rocks — whalers, wobbegongs, and grey nurses. Little Seal Rock is slightly smaller than Big Seal but the fish life here is reported to be more prolific.

The Cave at Big Seal Rock is the best place for sighting the grey nurse shark, often in packs of twenty to thirty. *The Cave* is actually an overhang above a large stage-like area: ideal for the photographer who wishes to get close to the sharks. The average depth is around 70 feet. *The Shark Hole* on the northeast tip of Big Seal Rock is also a common sighting place for grey nurse sharks at around 70 ft also. The surrounding walls are covered with invertebrate life. Moray eels inhabit the crevices from depth to the surface.

The quiet township of Nelson Bay at the entrance to Port Stephens is a popular holiday destination with all facilities. The Myall Lakes system extends from the harbor all the way up to Seal Rocks, and is a popular area for safe cruising. Offshore diving is excellent with many sites nearby at the entrance to the harbor, rocky headlands and offshore reefs, and wrecks.

Fly Point is an excellent shore dive, located at the northern end of Nelson Bay. The reef is covered in sponges, anemones, branching hydroids, and some tropical corals. The *Fly Point–Halifax Park Marine Reserve* extends 500 meters between Nelson Bay and Shoal Bay. The Aquatic

The solitary hydroid (Family Tubulariidae) attaches itself to rocky reefs and feeds on plankton and suspended sediments. The magnificent hydroid (Ralpharia magnifica) grows up to two inches in diameter on a stem up to five inches. Hydroids are common in all Australian temperate waters.

Reserve is an excellent dive, one of the most popular in the area, with rocky terrain and diverse invertebrate species and fishes.

Broughton Island is just a short trip north of Port Stephens by boat and the most popular dive site in the region, with superb marine life and many sheltered bays so that a lee is always available. The huge sea caves at the southern end of the island are fascinating, even if you are not diving. There are more than a dozen documented dive sites around the main island and its smaller islets and reef, all with prolific marine life and the usual range of temperate water reef and pelagic species.

The industrial city of Newcastle is the sixth-largest city in Australia. Population is just over a quarter million. There are several dive shops in the greater Newcastle region servicing sites north and south of the city. Oyster Banks, at the northern entrance to Newcastle Harbour, has claimed a dozen wrecks and more than a hundred lives during the past century.

Further south from Newcastle, the old mining town of Catherine Hill Bay is particularly interesting, with its old wharf and miners' cottages. There is good diving around the old jetty and off the rocks to the east at Desoto Inlet.

Catterthun *and* Satara *Wrecks*

Nearly two miles north of Seal Rocks is a reef with one of the most interesting wrecks in Australia. The 2179-ton steamship *Catterthun* sank during a storm in August, 1895, taking with her sixty-one passengers and crew, and 11,000 pounds (currency) in gold sovereigns bound for China. In 1896, hard hat divers, in spite of the depths and primitive gear of the day, managed to salvage most of the sovereigns. The ship lies across a sloping seabed with its portside at a depth of 170 feet. Two large engine block mounts reach up to a depth of 150 feet.

Just fifteen years after the *Catterthun* went down, the 5272-ton British India Company steamer *Satara* went down just southwest of Little Seal Rock. No lives were lost. The ship was discovered in September, 1984. She lies virtually intact on sand in 140 feet. Like the *Catterthun*, she is swarming with fish, but the depth and local conditions make the two wrecks suitable for the advanced deep diver only.

Greater Sydney

Typical depth range:	10-120 feet
Typical current conditions:	None to moderate
Expertise required:	Novice to experienced
Access:	Mainly boat, some shore diving

With a population of four million, Sydney is Australia's largest city. It is located on one of the finest natural harbors in the world and has a unique skyline dominated by the Sydney Harbour Bridge, the famous Opera House, and the futuristic Centrepoint Tower. Towering steel and glass buildings testify to the prosperity of the city.

Sydney has many dive shops spread throughout the suburbs, the coastal resorts, and many inland provincial centers. There is excellent diving within easy travelling distance from both northern and southern suburbs. The entrances to Port Jackson, Botany Bay, and Port Hacking are good on a calm day and a few hours' driving will bring the diver within reach of Jervis Bay to the south and Nelson Bay to the north. Charter trips arranged by Sydney diveshops are available to nearby locations as well as distant weekend trips.

Spectacular, dramatic, and controversial, the Sydney Opera house took fourteen years to build at a cost of $100 million. It was finally opened in 1974.

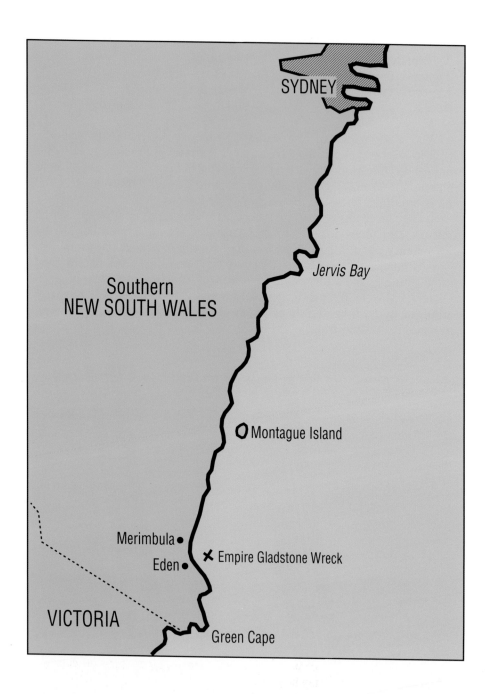

SYDNEY

Jervis Bay

Southern
NEW SOUTH WALES

⭕ Montague Island

Merimbula ●

Eden ● ✖ Empire Gladstone Wreck

VICTORIA

Green Cape

Broken Bay lies at the northern extremity of greater Sydney; it is another of the state's magnificent waterways. Further north is Terrigal, a popular holiday town just 60 miles by road from the Sydney Harbour Bridge. Terrigal is a favorite due to its accessibility and varied diving. There are several diveable wrecks in the area and the reefs are quite interesting with small caves, crevices, and the occasional drop-off. Fish life is prolific and the terrain is covered in sponges and invertebrates. Dive locations include *Foggy* and *Forresters* reefs and *Skillion* with its underwater caves and crevices down to 60 feet. The sheltered Terrigal Haven is quite worthwhile, with all-weather diving and plenty of schooling fish.

Some of Sydney's hundreds of popular dive sites in the greater Sydney region have quaint names such as Old Man's Hat, Perfume Point, Cabbage Tree Wall, Curl Curl Reef, Wedding Cake Island, Black Streak Reef, Rosa Gully, Jibbon Bombora, and Sea Dragons. The many wrecks are more sombre: the *Dunbar, Annie M. Miller, Valiant, Birchgrove Park, Catherine Adamson, SS Duckenfield,* and *Tuggerah,* among others.

Shiprock (at the entrance to Dolans Bay inside Port Hacking) is unique in its variety of marine fauna. The 30-ft swim out from shore takes you over a shallow sandy bottom to a steep dropoff whose face is covered in marine life — many different species of hydroids, sponges, and beautiful white-polyped telesto; sea anemones and feather duster worms in millions

A bright yellow gorgonia sea fan struggles for space on a rock wall covered in algae, ascidians, and sponges.

cover every square inch of the wall. A small area has been declared an Aquatic Reserve.

An extensive reef extends half a mile on the Pacific Ocean side of *South Head*. Depth varies from 30 to 90 ft to a sandy bottom. The reef is riddled with small caves and crevices, and huge round and flat rocks have fallen from the sheer vertical cliffs. Sponges, nudibranchs, and invertebrates are common, as is kelp. *Long Reef Point,* off the Griffith Golf Course at Dee Why, extends like a hooked thumb into the south Pacific Ocean. Being on suburbia's doorstep, it is a popular shore dive for snorkelers and scuba divers. The reef runs for about a mile offshore with a vertical drop-off wall extending from 15 ft down to 60 ft for about 200 yards. Marine life here is excellent, particuarly ascidians, sponges, hydroids, and solitary corals. The reef is an Aquatic Reserve.

There are no less than ten hulks scuttled on *Ship Reef,* an artificial reef some three miles offshore from Narrabeen Head, north of the entrance to Sydney Harbour. It is said that the reef was formed for line fishermen only, the thinking being that at 150 feet it was too deep for scuba divers. But it has proved to be a most interesting and popular site for divers despite the depth, which is not excessive under the right conditions and training. The most popular hulk is the famous Manly ferry *Dee Why*. She was scuttled in 1976 after completing her last run in 1968 and now sits upright on a sandy bottom with interesting swim-throughs over her 200-ft length.

Sydney's Favorite Wreck

Sydney's best known wreck crashed onto rocks at the Gap on South Head in 1857. Of 122 people on board the migrant clipper ship *Dunbar*, only one survived. Many beautiful artifacts have been recovered, including gold sovereigns, silver and copper coins, pennies, diamond engagement rings, gold wedding rings, gold watches and dentures, telescopes, and compasses. The wreck site is marked by the ballast blocks and anchors, but it is in shallow water that the small items are to be found. Naturally, the weather has to be perfect for a dive on this spot. The wreck has been declared a Historic Shipwreck.

Miami Trench off Cape Banks is covered in sponges and hydroids with prolific fish life and a variety of nudibranchs. The bottom consists of a covering of large boulders and gutters, and a wall of some 20 ft. Maximum depth is 80 ft. *Henry's Head* is a popular night dive and novice area, with good shallow diving on ledges and gutters. Large cuttlefish and squid are frequently seen.

Bat Ray Reef at the southern entrance to Botany Bay has a fine sponge garden over terraced steps down to 80 ft. Port Jackson sharks and schooling fish are common. *Osbourne Shoals* begins with a sandy bottom at 80 ft and rises in a series of steps — one of the best dives in Port Hacking.

Fish Reef is a small patch covered in sea whips and hovering school fish. It's one of the best dives south of Sydney. There is fine reef diving at *Marley Point* with excellent marine life including leafy seadragons, Port Jackson sharks, and the opportunity to see huge sunfish.

The heavily industrialized Greater Wollongong area fifty miles south of Sydney includes several towns. The largest steelworks in Australia is located at Port Kembla.

The Five Islands southeast of Wollongong drop down to about 50 ft and are known for their fish life. Just off Toothbrush Island is the wreck of the collier *Bombo* lost in 1949 and only discovered in 1975. The fore and aft sections of the broken hull lie upside down in 100 ft and are popular dives. *Wollongong Reef,* due east of the town, drops from 60 ft

Below these menacing cliffs lies one of Australia's most famous shipwrecks. In 1857, the wooden clipper Dunbar *crashed into jagged rocks and sank with the loss of the full complement except for one lone sailor. The site is popular with Sydney divers. Although protected by the Historic Shipwreck Act, small artifacts such as coins and buttons are still found among the rocks.*

down to 120 ft and is covered with the usual temperate water growth of sponges, gorgonia, anemones, and hydroids. The reef is alive with pelagics including schooling tuna and kingfish.

Bellambi Reef, north of Wollongong, is known as the Ship's Graveyard. Two dozen ships have been dumped here between 1859 and as recently as 1949. Most have broken up, providing only the pleasures that wreck scavengers would know, but the area is a good dive. The reef juts out from Bellambi Point and on the eastern side goes down to about 60 feet.

Out of the Fog

On April 2, 1931, Sydney was enveloped in heavy fog. Two fishermen sat in a rowboat anchored not far from shore, fishing during the early hours of the morning. One of the men looked up and sat speechless as a huge passenger ship steamed between them and the shore. When the fog lifted, the 4,500-ton passenger liner *Malabar* was aground on the rocks at Long Bay Headland between Botany Bay and Port Jackson. All passengers were removed during the calm weather and a cargo of finches escaped later, multiplying under the ideal conditions in Australia to such proportions as to become pests. The weather deteriorated and the ship became a total loss within twenty-four hours. A dive on the 350-ft wreck is quite interesting as tons of machinery, winches, hull plates, and fittings lie scattered over a vast area in only 30 ft of water. The huge engine block and a massive prop shaft are impressive.

They are to be found under any jetty — schools of old wives (Enoplosus armatus). *Photo courtesy of Chris and Cathy Deane, Adelaide.*

Jervis Bay

Typical depth range:	20-60 ft
Typical current conditions:	None within the bay
Expertise required:	Novice to experienced
Access:	Boat

Jervis Bay, 120 miles south of Sydney, is one of the most popular dive destinations in Australia, with excellent facilities, dive shops, dive charter services, and a range of accommodations including motels and dive lodges. Huskisson is the main town center.

Jervis Bay is to many Australian divers (particularly those from Sydney and Canberra) one of the finest regions for prolific temperate-water marine life and interesting terrain. Main town Huskisson is a busy fishing port and popular holiday base.

The bright yellow colouring of Nepanthia troughtoni *stands out on the algae-covered reef in its southern Australian habitat, but the animal is relatively uncommon.*

The bay is enclosed by Point Perpendicular to the north and Bowen Island to the south, and surrounded by white sandy beaches except for an occasional rocky headland. Brilliant invertebrates, superb sponge gardens, and interesting terrain make the bay popular. Whales are occasionally seen. For the most part, the best diving is along the ocean coastline.

To the south, from Bowen Island down to Summercloud Bay, stretches some of the deepest and most exciting diving to be found anywhere along the east coast of Australia.

Summercloud Bay has excellent shore diving, particularly at the western end during north-easterlies, with depths to 50 feet. *Green Patch* provides good snorkelling or a shallow scuba dive. *Smuggler's Cave* is a great dive with calm waters but the surge can be dangerous within the cave.

The terrain is fascinating, down to 60 ft. *Crocodile Head* is the northeast point of the headland and is a good dive down to 120 ft with sheer walls.

The Arch is perhaps the most popular of Jervis Bay dives, a natural underwater rock bridge at 120 ft covered in marine life. Blue grouper and wobbegong sharks are generally found under the Arch. *Point Perpendicular* is the northern headland to the Jervis Bay entrance and has excellent fish life.

The Docks is an excellent dive, usually protected, just inside the heads on the northern side of the bay. There is a long crevice at the western end and swim-throughs at the eastern with small caves covered in marine growth; brilliant for invertebrate macro-photography. Depths extend to 60 feet.

Currarong and *Honeymoon Bay* on the northern headland have shallow reefs for spearfishing and crays as well as deep reefs and wrecks for the scuba diver.

A large steamship, the *Merimbula,* lies directly in front of Merimbula Point. It's within easy reach of rockhoppers and a good anchorage for boat divers.

Bushranger's Bay

Bass Point juts out into the Pacific Ocean south of Shellharbour, 50 miles north of Jervis Bay, forming the northern headland to Bushranger's Bay. The bay features drop-offs and reef with kelp forests, and is a nursery habitat for juvenile fish. *The Arch*, just south of the southern headland, is an excellent dive with prolific marine life around the entrance. The walls and ceiling of the cave are covered in invertebrates — sponges, gorgonia, sea tulips, and feather dusters. Maximum depth past the entrance is 100 ft but the bay itself is rather shallow with excellent sponge gardens. The wrecks of the *Alexander Berry* and *City Service Boston* lie just offshore from the north end of the point.

Southern Coast, New South Wales

Typical depth range:	20-110 ft
Typical current conditions:	Can be strong
Expertise required:	Intermediate to experienced (remote regions)
Access:	Boat, shore, and jetty

The southern New South Wales coast from Ulladulla down to Green Cape is most attractive with delightful coastal towns and a pleasant climate. Each major town has a dive operator, usually with full charter facilities. The diving is temperate — some have likened it to the California coast. Conditions can vary considerably as this is an open stretch of coast facing the Pacific Ocean. There are, however, many secluded bays which have a lee shore. The best diving, particularly for pelagics and clear water, is in the open ocean on inshore reefs or off the nearby islands. Underwater visibility is around 100 ft when seas are flat and there has been little or no rainfall for two weeks or so.

Rocky reef platforms and protruding headlands line the south-central New South Wales coast, ideal terrain for fisherman and diver alike. Offshore reefs are readily accessible from the many coastal villages, while shore diving is popular on a calm day.

Sponges of all shapes, sizes, and colors are common in all Australian waters.

Ulladulla. The picturesque fishing village of Ulladulla and the neighboring town of Milton lie south of Jervis Bay, only three hours' drive from either Sydney or Canberra. The region is popular for its beautiful lakes and lagoons, sandy white beaches, and near perfect climate. Shore diving is excellent but limited by a rugged coastline and lack of suitable access roads, hence boat diving from Ulladulla is more convenient.

Lighthouse Reef juts out of the sea less than half a mile east of Warden Head Lighthouse on the southern approaches to Ulladulla harbor, runs south for half a mile parallel to the mainland, and then gradually disappears underwater. The reef has a protected lee side making it popular for boat diving. Out beyond the reef wall, huge boulders scattered over the seabed are covered in sea tulips, gorgonia, hydroids, sponges, and tall sea whips. Fish life is prolific. Magnificent leafy sea dragons are often found in pairs amongst the dense growth.

Other excellent sites include *Mindbenders Reef, Burrill Rocks Reef,* and the wreck of the clipper ship *Walter Hood* which can be found halfway between Ulladulla and Jervis Bay. Wrecked in 1870, very little remains of the *Walter Hood*.

Brush Island. Tiny, uninhabited Brush Island lies fifty minutes by boat south of Ulladulla, and is a wildlife and nature reserve with an automatic lighthouse on the eastern side. A reef off Brush Island runs in a northeast direction down to 100 ft, providing unusual sponge gardens and bommies. Strong currents run here.

Diving all around Brush Island is interesting, particularly on the sheltered northern side where there are ruins of an old wreck in about 50 ft, more than likely from the 200-tonne freighter *Northern Firth,* one of two ships known to have gone down off the island. The French-built barque *Camden* went down between Brush Island and the mainland in January, 1870, and for many years her hull was a well-known landmark. She gradually deteriorated and now only parts of the superstructure and deck can be seen underwater.

Batemans Bay. This is another popular dive and holiday location, 188 miles south of Sydney. Shore access is generally limited due to the rugged coastline and lack of suitable roads, but boat diving opens up many diving sites.

The Tunnel is a popular dive: a cave system about 15 ft in diameter and extending for about 60 ft where light enters through a vertical chimney. *The Arch* is another excellent dive, with an entrance covered in marine growth harboring crayfish and reef fish. Other popular sites include *The Chimney, Black Rock,* and *Tollgate Island,* and the wreck of the 200-ton *John Penn* off Broulee, 15 miles south of Batemans Bay.

Montague Island. Montague Island is only a short boat ride from Narooma. It is one of the most beautiful islands off the eastern Australian coast and popular for its magnificent marine life and good underwater visibility. The island is a sanctuary, hence landing on the island is not permitted. This has encouraged an active seal population. Good diving can be had in depths from 30 ft down to around 100 ft, although it drops down to 300 ft on the northeast tip. Strong currents frequently whip around the island.

Montague Island is popular during the Australian summer as big schools of trevally, kingfish, and tuna move into the area around the new year. *Shark Gutter* is a fissure running off the island into deep water where grey nurse sharks are frequently seen. Some of the better diving is from the seal colony at the northern end of the island, and around the west side down toward the wharf and boatshed, about halfway down the western side.

Aughinish Rock lies two miles southwest of Montague. South of the reef lies the wreck of the 780-tonne collier *Lady Darling,* lost in 1880. Aughinish Reef does not break the surface, coming up from 100 ft to within 10 ft of the surface. The outer seaward side has the better diving, with steep drop-off walls covered in sponges, corals, and other invertebrate life, and prolific reef fish and pelagic species.

You couldn't help but love these gorgeous creatures. This inquisitive fellow had probably never seen a human before.

Bermagui. Bermagui is a quiet holiday village eleven miles south of Narooma. *Gorgonian Patch* provides a colorful dive in 30 ft of water. Sheltered by the Bermagui headland, the reef is diveable in most weather conditions and is easily accessible from the shore. Gorgonian corals and large schools of pelagic fish are the attractions.

Blue Pool Bombora breaks the surface some 300 yards offshore and drops quickly to a depth of 50 ft where the bottom is a profusion of color — Gorgonian coral, many different kinds of sponges, sea tulips, and ascidians. Fish include red morwong, hulafish, and various species of wrasse. Further seaward, where the bottom shelves to 80 ft, lies an area of superb reef with a range of species from the temperate water leafy sea dragon to tropical lionfish and splendid perch. At the outer edge of the reef is a drop-off from 80 to 110 feet with a forest of sea whips.

Tathra. Located on a beautiful rugged coastline, the holiday village of *Tathra* has excellent shore diving and snorkelling with gutters, caves, and sponge gardens. Local dive operators regard the sites near to the Tathra boat ramp as being some of the best for temperate marine life in Australia. Weedy sea dragons are frequently seen. The best sites include *Little Kangarutha, Big Kangarutha, The Gutters, Tathra Head Bommie,*

Temperate-water gorgonia sea fans tend to be smaller than their tropical cousins, but no less colorful.

and *The Pressure Points*. There is excellent shore diving near Tathra's historic *Steamer Wharf*, and *Kianniny Bay*. This section of the coastline is also known for its superb fishing.

Merimbula. Merimbula is a popular holiday resort with motel and dive lodge accommodation, and excellent boat and shore diving. The wreck of the *Empire Gladstone* is only a short boat ride south, off Haystack Rock. There is excellent shore diving near the *Merimbula Wharf,* and off *Yellow Rock* further north, *Short Point,* and *Tura Head.*

One of the best wrecks in the locality is the 7,090-ton freighter *Empire Gladstone.* She struck near Haystack Rock off Pambula in 1950 and, although well and truly broken up, parts of her at least still resemble a ship. The 429-ft ship was on her way from Adelaide to Sydney carrying a cargo of car bodies and iron ore valued at three quarters of a million Australian pounds when she hit the reef.

Merimbula on the south central New South Wales coast is a popular holiday and retirement town nestled between shallow Merimbula Lake and Merimbula Bay. There is excellent boat and shore diving nearby.

Eden. The former old whaling town of Eden is an active fishing port with fine boating on Twofold Bay, a natural protected harbor. The Whaling Museum has on display the skeleton of the famous killer whale named Tom, a legend in whaling folklore.

Eden has always been a popular diving holiday location, with excellent motel and camping facilities, and easy access to Green Cape and the Ben Boyd National Park. There is good all-weather diving, both from shore and with a boat, with miles of rocky coastline, sheltered bays, and headlands.

Two ocean-going tugs, the *Henry Bolte* and *Tasman Hauler* have been scuttled in 60 to 90 ft just south of Twofold Bay, not far from the historic Boyd's Tower. The wrecks are proving to be excellent artificial reefs.

Green Cape. Green Cape juts out into the Pacific Ocean halfway between the Victorian border and Eden, a national park having spectacular coastal scenery with remote inlets and dense forest. The Green Cape Lighthouse is at the far tip of the Cape. Disaster Bay lies to the south and Twofold Bay further north toward Eden.

It's a rare day when you cannot dive Green Cape, with a lee shore either on the north or the south side. It is shore diving at its best. Tracks

"Bazza" the Blue Grouper (Achoerodus viridis) *is tame enough to be hand-fed by divers. His home is off the Merimbula Wharf in southern New South Wales. Photo courtesy of Dave Warth.*

lead through the forest, sometimes to a car park and picnic ground, other times to a remote seemingly deserted bay. It is not unusual to have to carry dive gear for a mile or so — worth every agonizing step. For the best locations, talk to the local divers, or better still, dive with a local operator. Good drop-offs with abundant fish life and good visibility make the area very popular. The northern side offers the best diving, with 60 ft of water straight off the rocky shore at most places. The southern side offers variety with shallower areas shelving out into deeper water. A visit to the lighthouse is a must, and also the cemetery where those who lost their lives on the wreck of the *Ly-Ee-Moon* off the lighthouse are buried.

During the late summer months large schools of pelagic fish move around the Cape and it is possible to see huge yellowfin tuna, southern

Green Cape Lighthouse sits on a promontory separating Disaster Bay from the Tasman Sea. At the base of the cliffs lie the remains of the ill-fated Lye-Ee-Moon, *wrecked in 1886 with the loss of seventy-one lives.*

bluefin tuna, yellowtail kingfish, and perhaps the occasional bronze whaler shark.

Mowarry Point is a prominent rocky point between Green Cape and the South Head of Twofold Bay. Mowarry is typical of southeast coast diving, with its white boulders stepping down to a rocky bottom at 60 ft. Fish life here is best in summer months, particularly for huge schools of trevally, mackerel, sweep, and pike. Wobbegong sharks, blue morwong, and green wrasse are common.

Eden, overlooking magnificent Twofold Bay, is southern New South Wales' oldest town, starting as a whaling port in the 1840s. It is now a prosperous fishing village and holiday destination.

4

Victoria Coast

Wilsons Promontory

Typical depth range: 20-110 ft
Typical current conditions: Can be very strong
Expertise required: Experienced, due to remoteness and
                                          varying conditions
Access: Boat

Driving onto Wilsons Promontory is like entering another world. After passing through the rolling hills of West Gippsland you arrive at "The Prom" with its mountains of solid granite and heavily timbered hills. Offshore islands jut out of the blue ocean waters of Bass Strait.

Granite rock formations extend down to the seabed off Wilsons Promontory, providing the substructure for prolific temperate marine life.

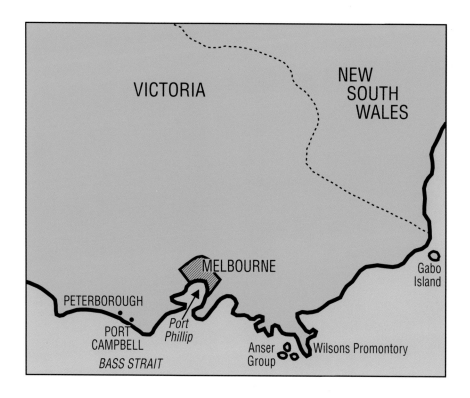

Below water, Wilsons Promontory is equally spectacular. The tall granite cliffs and large boulders which can be seen all along the coast descend into the sea to form immense caves, deep ledges, and spectacular drop-offs. It is the perfect dive location and the perfect habitat for a diversity of marine plants and animals. Solitary hydroids, zoanthids, and gorgonia sea fans add color to exotic creatures such as the sea dragon and a number of nudibranch species.

The magnificent coves on the eastern coastline are accessible only by a day walk or by boat. Live-aboard charter boats out from Port Albert and Port Welshpool seek overnight refuge in Sealers Cove, Refuge Cove, and Waterloo Bay. As the region is a National Park, there are limited facilities; a general store, camping ground, and cabins are located at Tidal River, 136 miles southeast from Melbourne. The nearest airfill station and dive operator are at Inverloch, 60 miles toward Melbourne.

The Wilsons Promontory Marine Reserve creates a 300-meter-wide totally protected zone around the rocky reefs between Norman Bay and Refuge Cove. All types of amateur fishing, including angling, spearfishing, and diving for abalone and rock lobster are prohibited in the area.

Awesome Kanowna Island stands 360 ft high off Wilsons Promontory, the huge cave providing its popular name of Skull Rock. Cannon balls have been found in the cave.

Without a powerful cruiser, your base camp will have to be Tidal River, as the distances from Port Welshpool, Sandy Point, and Walkerville South are too great for small boats. Offshore islands vary in distance from Tidal River, with excellent diving at Shellback Island (6 miles), Norman Island (3 miles), and the Glennies (4 miles). Small boats can be launched from the beach at Tidal River. A permit is required.

Although it could be expected that at least one side of the peninsula would have a lee shore, that is not always the case. Seas are always southerly, and whereas offshore winds may make for an easy trip to nearby islands, the return trip may be difficult, indeed hazardous.

For the rock hopper, areas are limited, with *Tongue Point, Leonard Point, Pillar Point,* and *Norman Point* all offering good diving. Deep water (30-100 ft) is common with heavy kelp growth. The bottom is made up of big granite boulders which form huge caves and spectacular underwater scenery.

The Anser Group has excellent diving but, while just over a mile offshore, these islands are 7 miles from the nearest boat launching area at Tidal River. The group consists of *Anser, Kanowna,* and *Skull Rock* (or Cleft Island) and three smaller islands called the Anderson Islets. *Carpenters Reef* is a good dive on a calm day. *Anser Island* is droplet-shaped. Its pointed low northwest end rises to a peak of 400 ft in the southeast. Below the peak there is a small bay facing southwest that is well worth a dive. Massive granite slabs broken off from the island cliff over the centuries have landed haphazardly, making a number of large caves that are home to a variety of fish and invertebrates.

Most of the granite islands off Wilsons Promontory contain seal colonies. Thousands of animals mass together during the hectic breeding season.

There is nothing so awesome as approaching *Skull Rock* from a distance and seeing the huge cave loom into view high on the 360-ft tall rock. Cannon balls have been found in the cave; it appears that early sealers and sailing ship captains saw the cave as a target for artillery practice. Underwater, the rock plunges down to around 100 ft. The diving here is not so impressive, however, as the swells inhibit the opportunity for interesting invertebrate life. The area between the northeast side of Skull Rock and Kanowna Island is more interesting. The water is very deep here, from around 100 to 160 ft, often with a strong current running, but the water clarity and abundant marine life are superb. Some days the surface may appear cloudy from plankton, but down 30 ft the visibility improves dramatically as you enter clear blue water. The bottom is covered

Always seeking an audience, playing Australian fur seal pups will romp among divers and seem to pose for the underwater camera. The fur seal is common throughout southeast Australia, often gathering on islands in the thousands during breeding season.

Diving with Seals

Divers should be aware that seals must be approached with extreme caution while they are on dry land. Inside those puppylike lips are a formidable set of teeth capable of tearing a large piece of flesh from the overconfident visitor. The best approach is from the land side of the seal. Get no closer than 10 ft and make sure not to go between the seal and any means of escape, usually the water. Once in the water, the seals are generally quite harmless. They can be approached within inches, but they will more than likely approach you. They will also mimic your movements — if you lie on the bottom and blow bubbles, then they will do so also — if you duck, dive, twist, and turn, then they will follow suit. But be cautious at all times and treat them gently. A cow seal may dart at a diver if she thinks there is an element of danger to her cubs. But rarely will the cow actually make contact with the diver.

And a particular word of caution: Seals are on the menu for the white pointer shark and several diver attacks have taken place in known great white shark feeding grounds. If those playful seals you have been cavorting with suddenly disappear, you may have cause for concern. If you are near the bottom, stay there, and observe the surroundings. At the earliest apparently safe opportunity, make your way back to shore or the boat, exit promptly, and do not return to the area that day.

with huge boulders some 60 ft tall covered with a variety of invertebrates — sponges, soft corals, ascidians, bryozoans, and zoanthids.

Kanowna Island, named after the ship that ran aground and sank near the island in 1929, is a seal colony. Kanowna has two bays facing east where the rocks slope gently into the sea. At the height of the breeding season, thousands of Australian Fur Seals gather here; do not dive during November and December. The southeast tip of the island also has spectacular walls with prolific fish and invertebrate life.

Great Glennie Island has fine diving, especially Ramsbotham Rocks off the northern tip of the island which slopes to a sandy bottom at 65 ft.

The northwest tip and the western tip of *Norman Island* are the best regions for diving, and also within the small cove on the western side. Fish life is prolific here with long-snouted boarfish, old wives, and a variety of wrasse.

Port Phillip

Typical depth range:	20-120 ft
Typical current conditions:	Can be strong
Expertise required:	Intermediate to experienced
Access:	Boat

Port Phillip Bay is roughly diamond-shaped, with Melbourne, the second largest city in Australia, at its northern apex and a narrow entrance at the southern end. Melbourne has beautiful gardens, wide streets, electric tramcars, and some of the finest Federation (turn of the century) architecture in Australia. It is headquarters of Australian Rules Football, and the Melbourne Cup. The northern region of the bay has no diving of note — Melburnians head south for excellent diving.

The southern region of Port Phillip is a most delightful holiday region with generally mild but sometimes unpredictable weather. Perfect conditions are required to dive outside the narrow entrance called "The Heads." The narrow passage of water between the headlands known as The Rip has brought many a ship to its final resting place. The diving in The Rip

Melbourne is one of the few cities in the world with a significant electric tramcar network, greatly reducing inner-city pollution. The garden city at the head of Port Phillip is known for its excellent shopping, superb cuisine, and cultural nightlife.

is brilliant but is restricted to slack tide in perfect seas. Drift diving takes advantage of the strong flood current into the bay.

Southern Port Phillip consists of two peninsulas forming the entrance to the bay, like huge pincers. The eastern tip is Point Nepean, at the end of the Mornington Peninsula. This is an extremely popular region with rolling hills and a dozen seaside resorts. The last village "at the end of the road" is Portsea, 70 miles south from Melbourne. The western head is Point Lonsdale just south of the beautiful historic town of Queenscliff, 66 miles by road from Melbourne through Geelong. Portsea and Queenscliff are the diving centers, with several dive charter operators and excellent diver lodge accommodation, as well as motels and guest houses. The region offers exhilarating diving, particularly for the wreck diver and underwater photographer, with extensive reefs and a variety of shipwrecks.

Lonsdale Reef is honeycombed with caves and ledges and is the graveyard for more than fifty shipwrecks. It is particularly noted for its variety of nudibranchs. The reef needs a low tide on the ebb backed up by no swell. Although access from shore is possible, it is safe to dive only from a boat in case a current takes the diver away from shore. Good snorkelling can be had in the bight between Point Lonsdale and Queenscliff, but care should be taken with the current. This whole area is riddled with caves and ledges, large crayfish, and countless fish.

Lonsdale Wall offers some of the most spectacular underwater terrain in Australia. The Wall starts at The Rip and extends into the bay for half a mile. The wall consists of a series of escarpments and undercut ledges. Covered by fronds of strap kelp, the reef at 30 ft quickly drops off to several ledges, then plunges to a depth of over 200 ft. At 60 ft, zoanthids, sponges, soft corals, and huge bryozoan colonies thrive in the current conditions. Schools of butterfly perch surround divers; long-snouted

Strong tidal currents and the nutrients they carry have led to a profusion of marine life at the southern end of Port Phillip. An added attraction is that the area is continually flushed with clear water from Bass Strait, and on average, good to excellent visibility can be obtained year-round. Needless to say the best diving occurs following a flood tide. The tidal currents are responsible for the marine life in the area, but they also impose restrictions on the diver. The slack water periods present a 30 minute window of opportunity for divers to explore the reef, free of the overpowering currents. Most of the dive locations inside the Port Phillip Heads area are affected by the tidal currents.

Portsea, idyllic holiday resort for the rich and famous, is also a major departure point for dive boats visiting sites near Port Phillip heads.

boarfish, blue-throated wrasse, and blue devil fish prowl the open reef. Past 100 ft an incredible garden of delicate corals, jewel anemones, hydroids, and sea whips cover the reef.

The *Point Nepean Rock Platform* on the eastern side of The Rip is similar to Point Lonsdale. Land approach is restricted, as this is a Defense Reserve, however, sea access is no problem. The submerged reefs on both sides of Point Nepean have superb underwater terrain, but the strong currents in this area can be very dangerous. *Quarantine Bay* lies directly behind Point Nepean inside Port Phillip and offers some protection on an interesting limestone reef.

As the name suggests, *The Kelp Beds* are recognizable at low tide by the huge fronds of kelp floating on the surface, but the bottom is where the action is. Ledges and caves provide homes for many species of fish and during the summer months big schools of pelagic fish frequent the area.

Located in the tidal stream of The Rip, *Portsea Hole* less than a mile from the Portsea Pier is a series of ledges that step from a depth of 40 ft to a deep sandy bottom at 80 ft. There are bold blue devils, kingsized leatherjackets, barber and butterfly perch, gurnards, goatfish, and jackass morwong, along with almost every other variety of southern marine fish

Drift diving is popular at the southern end of the bay. From a line attached to a boat or a large buoy, divers can drift with the current with relative safety. This is exhilarating diving and a vast amount of territory can be covered. It has also proved to be very rewarding for bottle collectors, with many old and prized specimens being obtained.

that divers expect to find in Victorian waters. The ledges are covered in prolific growth of giant finger sponges, bryozoans, hydroids, zoanthids and ascidians, tangled tube worms, spindly sea spiders, and brightly colored nudibranchs. Even the old pylons of *Portsea Pier* support a diverse invertebrate community.

Originally intended last century as a fortress against enemy shipping entering the Bay, *Pope's Eye Annulus* is a man-made semi-circular ring of bluestone rocks rising up about six feet from sea on the crown of Pope's Eye Shoal, two miles inside Port Phillip Bay. The never-completed fortification was initially constructed as a mooring for Victoria's warship *Cerberus* and now provides an artificial reef for marine plants and animals. Constant water movement keeps the reef well supplied with plankton and dissolved oxygen. As a result, Pope's Eye supports a richness and diversity

Taking a firm grip on a reef ledge to avoid being swept away with the surge, kelp "roots" compete for space with sponges, corals, ascidians, and algae.

This is one of six J-Class submarines in the Port Phillip region, now a breakwater at Swan Island. Four others lie in deep water south of the Heads and are popular dives.

A dozen ships lie off the Port Nepean rock platform at the eastern entrance to Port Phillip, known as the notorious Rip. Seas here can be treacherous, hence diving is limited to the rare calm day.

of marine life unique in Port Phillip Bay. On the seaward side, high current flow encourages heavy growths of such filter-feeding sedentary animals as sponges, corals, sea fans, bryozoa, and sea squirts.

Port Phillip has several interesting shipwrecks. The most popular is the three-masted iron barque *Eliza Ramsden,* which sank in the South Channel in 1875 after striking Corsair Rock at the entrance to Port Phillip. The wreck lies upright in 60 ft and is in remarkably good condition despite being dynamited to give shipping clearance; its bow rises 20 ft from the seabed. During the summer, schools of yellowtail, kingfish, and trevally travel into the bay and are frequently seen in the area of the wreck.

Ship's Graveyard

Thirty-two vessels were scuttled during the 1920s and 1930s in an area several miles southwest of Port Phillip Heads. It is charted officially as foul ground, but the depth of greater than 100 ft makes it less of a shipping hazard. Commercial dive boats must be appropriately registered to be able to pass through Port Phillip Heads with divers aboard.

The most popular wreck is that of the 1,777-ton steel screw steamer *Rotomahana,* built in 1879 and scuttled in 1928. There are also four *J Class Submarines* of 1,260 tons built in 1916 and scuttled during 1926 and 1927. One of the subs is in 140 ft of water. It is sitting upright, is intact, and measures more than two hundred feet long. The submarine may be entered carefully. It is surrounded by prolific growth.

Important Note: The Ship's Graveyard and the J4 Submarines are for experienced divers only. The depth and open sea conditions make the dive potentially dangerous.

The seaward side of *Mornington Peninsula* provides superb shore diving off a magnificent rugged coastline, but it is not without its dangers. It was here, off Cheviot Beach, that Prime Minister Harold Holt was lost while diving in 1967. Places offering the best diving are *London Bridge, St Paul's Road, Diamond Bay, Canterbury Jetty Road,* and *Koonya Back Beach.* Calcarenite rock platforms deeply undercut by the sea form large caverns. Sponges and gorgonian fans grow from the walls of the caves. Long-snouted boarfish, banded morwong, and bullseye and magpie morwong are encountered on every dive. Fronds of giant kelp and bull kelp hang from above like curtains, adding an air of mystery.

The Shipwreck Coast

Typical depth range:	20-60 ft
Typical current conditions:	Frequent high and unpredictable ocean swells and strong currents are a major problem
Expertise required:	Experienced and advanced only
Access:	Boat

More than two hundred ships were wrecked along the 80-mile coastline from Cape Otway to Warrnambool during the second half of the nineteenth century when the Australian gold rush saw an influx of immigrants from England. Passenger and cargo ships sailing east on the Great Circle Route south of the Cape of Good Hope had to "thread the eye of the needle" before entering Bass Strait and proceeding to Melbourne and Sydney. The "Eye," between Cape Wickham on the northern tip of King Island and Cape Otway, is only 56 miles wide. This was a formidable target

The western Victorian coastline between Cape Otway and Warrnambool has some of the most spectacular scenery in Australia. Diving is limited due to the unpredictable nature of southern seas rolling in from Antarctica.

Diver Peter Ronald found this superb diamond and gold ring whilst diving on the site of the wrecked ship Schomberg *off Peterborough. The ring is on display at the Flagstaff Hill Maritime Village in Warrnambool where Ronald is now the curator.*

for an old-time ship with only simple navigational aids to locate after crossing 2,000 miles of southern ocean without sight of land. Too far south and vessels would pile up on the rocks of King Island; too far north and the hostile cliffs of western Victoria, despite their beauty, blocked ships' paths with disastrous results.

The coast on either side of Port Campbell is stunning. Four-hundred-foot cliffs drop down to pounding surf and small bays. On a good day, the diving close to shore is excellent — but good days are rare. Shore and boat diving is superb, but unpredictable and often dangerous. The southern winds can whip the sea into a frenzy at short notice, making it difficult to schedule charter boat trips.

The wreck of the *Loch Ard* is the main attraction to divers. She lies off Mutton Bird Island in a very open and treacherous area. Some of the wreckage and cargo of the historic ship is still in the gorge, but well buried in the sand. The area is also excellent for crayfishing and general scenic diving.

The quiet holiday village of *Peterborough* attracts many visiting divers over the holidays and weekends. Areas accessible by shore include *Schomberg Reef, Crofts Bay, Bay of Islands,* and *Childer's Cove.* All these areas offer good diving with crayfish being taken in relatively shallow

57

Flagstaff Hill Maritine Village at Warrnambool represents the early days of shipping in Australia.

water. The historic shipwrecks *Children, Schomberg, Newfield,* and *Antares* are all nearby. The *Falls of Halladale* is a good dive but do not attempt it from shore despite the temptation: it is too far to swim back if you get into difficulties.

Apart from being an excellent base for diving the western Victorian coastline, *Warrnambool* is gaining a reputation as an observation point for migrating whales from May to September. It is also the location of the finest maritime village and museum in Australia. Curator Peter Ronald has developed Flagstaff Hill Maritime Village as a faithful re-creation of a port as it was in the days of sail.

Diving with Whales

Whales are frequently seen off Warrnambool from May to September, however, diving is prohibited then as the whales are migrating to their breeding sites. Some may actually remain for several months within a small area near the town. It is an offense to pass in a boat within 200 meters of a whale, and an offense to dive, snorkel, or swim within 30 meters of a whale.

Victoria's Most Famous Shipwreck

The 1,623-ton sailing ship *Loch Ard* lies against rocks at the base of Mutton Bird Island, outside Loch Ard Gorge and east of Port Campbell. The *Loch Ard* made many successful voyages from England to Australia after its construction in 1873. On June 1, 1878, she crashed into rugged cliffs, leaving wreckage and bodies strewn along the coastline. Only two of the 51 passengers and crew on board were saved. Eva Carmichael lost her entire family as they were emigrating from England, and the only other survivor was ship's apprentice Tom Pierce, whose heroic efforts saved Miss Carmichael. The concept of rescue archaeology has been applied by the Maritime Archaeology Unit to the site of the *Loch Ard*. The wreck is scattered over a wide area at the base of sheer cliffs in 80 ft of water, and can only be visited in perfect conditions. Rescue archaeology entails recovery of threatened items on the site: (a) if they are unique and in better condition than existing material in landbased collections, or (b) if required for research and/or display.

The only two survivors from the ill-fated ship Loch Ard *were by chance washed into this gorge, the only one with a beach. The gorge now bears the name of the ship.*

Hardy kelp fronds cling to a reef substructure covered in algaes, sponges, and tiny seafans in a typical southern temperate-water scene.

Portland is the westernmost of Victoria's coastal towns, 50 miles east of the South Australian border, and is the only deep water port between Melbourne and Adelaide. Excellent diving is had at *Lawrence Rocks*, only a short boat ride out from Portland harbor. The terrain here is rugged, with superb kelp forests and prolific marine life.

5

South Australia Coast

Mount Gambier

Typical depth range:	10-120 + ft
Typical current conditions:	None
Expertise required:	Advanced/qualified to Cave Divers Association of Australia standards or acceptable equivalent
Access:	Shore

Mount Gambier is the largest South Australian town outside of Adelaide, and borders four extinct volcanoes which rise 600 ft above the surrounding plain. The largest of the four crater lakes, the magnificent

One Tree sinkhole is one of the most popular freshwater caverns in the Mount Gambier district. Like all the caves and caverns in the region, special cave diving qualifications are required before you are permitted to dive on private property or government land.

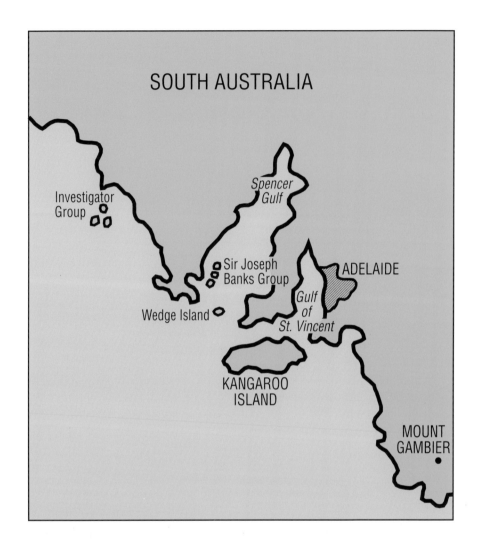

SOUTH AUSTRALIA

Spencer Gulf

Investigator Group

Sir Joseph Banks Group

Wedge Island

ADELAIDE

Gulf of St. Vincent

KANGAROO ISLAND

MOUNT GAMBIER

Blue Lake, is more than 600 ft deep and changes from a dull grey to a brilliant blue each November, reverting back to grey at the end of summer.

The Mount Gambier district has some of the finest freshwater sinkhole and cave diving in the world. The surrounding countryside is riddled with holes and caverns in the granite structure, most filled with crystal clear water. The sinkholes are on either private property or government land. You must have specific qualifications before permission is granted to dive in one of the 140 known sinkholes in this area. Most popular are *Piccaninny Ponds, Ewens Ponds, One Tree, Baby Blue, Eloh Elap, Gouldens,* and *Sisters.*

Ewens Ponds is one of the few sites where no permit or special qualifications are required, and this is an excellent scuba dive or snorkel for experienced or novice divers. Ewens Ponds consists of three large ponds connected via narrow open channels. Eels, freshwater crayfish, and several different species of fish inhabit the ponds, some permanently and others on an irregular basis, as the ponds eventually drain through the third and longest channel to the sea. Several species of saltwater fish are regularly seen in the ponds; they apparently swim in to rid themselves of parasites that cannot live in the fresh water. The juvenile stages of some common insects are also to be found amongst the abundance of algae growing in the top few feet of the ponds. The ponds are fed from both land runoff and underwater springs, and as a result the water is usually crystal clear, making for ideal diving and photography alike. Maximum depth is 35 ft, but most diving is done between 10 and 20 ft.

Piccanninny Ponds is the main attraction for most divers but the site is restricted to those who hold a Category 3 Cave Divers Qualification and have applied for and been granted the required permit to dive Picaninny. Snorkeling is allowed in "Pics" provided a permit is obtained from the National Parks and Wildlife Service in Mount Gambier. A 50-yard snorkel over the first pond leads to a vertical drop of more than 200 ft in the main chasm. This chamber is 160 ft long, but only 20 ft wide at the most. Visibility is incredible and the water a glorious blue. At 120 ft, the chasm narrows to a large tunnel that runs almost vertically down, and narrows dramatically with increasing depth. The water is exceptionally clear. At one end of the chasm, a large cave called *The Cathedral* drops down to 120 ft.

Diving Qualifications for Freshwater Sinkholes

Freshwater cave and sinkhole diving requires special skills gained through specific instruction, and meticulous preparation with the right equipment. Thirteen deaths have occurred in the sinkholes of Mount Gambier over the past two decades; crystal clear freshwater can be deceptive. Divers must be qualified according to Cave Divers Association of Australia requirements. Sinkholes are graded according to difficulty and safety. Divers must be qualified to the appropriate grading for the sinkholes they wish to enter. Most holes are on private land; some government-controlled holes such as Piccanninny Ponds require an additional permit to dive, snorkel, or swim. Some holes are also periodically closed for flora regeneration.

Overseas visitors should contact the Cave Divers Association of Australia, P.O. Box 1166, Mount Gambier, SA 5290, well in advance of traveling. State specific freshwater and/or cave diving skills, period of travel, and requirements. A permit is not required for an individual to dive Ewens Ponds, but permission is required for groups of six or more. Contact the Department of Lands, PMB 124, Mount Gambier, SA 5290. Phone: (087) 24 1598.

Kangaroo Island

Typical depth range:	20-60 ft
Typical current conditions:	Can be strong
Expertise required:	Intermediate to experienced
Access:	Ferry or plane to island, then shore or boat diving

Kangaroo Island is Australia's third-largest island, a fascinating wildlife area with superb beaches. The island is 90 miles long and roughly 30 miles wide. A vehicular ferry operates between Port Adelaide and Kingscote, and from Cape Jervis to Penneshaw. (Contact Tourism South Australia for details.) An airstrip provides a link with Adelaide airport.

The main town center is at Kingscote, with other towns at American River, Penneshaw, and Parndana. There are motels and guest house accommodations but no high-rise tourist developments. The western side of the island is remote, with no facilities.

No fewer than twelve conservation parks exist on the island. Native life flourishes because the island has no foxes or dingoes to attack small marsupials, and there are no rabbits to destroy the plant life.

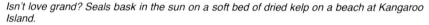

Isn't love grand? Seals bask in the sun on a soft bed of dried kelp on a beach at Kangaroo Island.

Delicate lace coral (Triphyllozoon monolifera) *is a prime example of how nature can create intricate patterns on an otherwise mundane terrain. This species is common on sheltered reefs and pylons in all Australian temperate waters.*

Seal Beach Aquatic Reserve, off the south coast of Kangaroo Island, has two zones, with public entry restricted in the western region to reduce human interference in the seal breeding colony. The eastern zone provides the opportunity to see the Australian Sea Lion *(Neophoca cinerea)*. Swimming is prohibited in Seal Bay.

The most outstanding feature of *Penneshaw jetty* is the large fans of gorgonia coral growing out from the wooden pylons in less than 20 ft. The jetty is a very safe dive, ideal for training or night diving. The Penneshaw Reef runs almost parallel to the jetty only about 100 ft away.

Kangaroo Head is just a few miles west of Penneshaw. The only access to the many small coves is by boat. The area is a photographer's delight with sponges, coral, and ascidians in abundance. It is here that explorer/navigator Matthew Flinders landed in 1802.

West Bay is probably most famous as the site of the historic shipwreck *Loch Vennachar,* a three-masted iron ship built in Glasgow. The wreck is just off a cliff about half a mile north of the bay, and is definitely not a dive for the inexperienced. Big swells rolling in from the southern ocean create hazardous surge conditions, particularly close to the cliffs. This dive is not on charter operators' itineraries, however, the bay itself deserves recognition as a good diving location. There are cliffs on both sides of the bay and reasonably calm water can be found on one side or the other.

A dive at *Cape Cassini* on the wreck sites of the *Fairfield* (1870) and *Brothers* (1912) is interesting. Nothing can be seen of the ships apart from the anchors of the *Fairfield* and large quantities of copper sheathing wedged between rocks. The relentless surge has covered most of the wreckage with sand.

Adelaide and Yorke Peninsula

Typical depth range:	10-80 ft
Typical current conditions:	Minor
Expertise required:	Novice to intermediate
Access:	Shore, jetty, and boat

Once called the City of Churches, more for its conservative attitudes than its architecture, Adelaide is now one of the liveliest state capitals in Australia, with excellent theatres and restaurants. The city center is completely surrounded by parks, and has examples of interesting nineteenth-century architecture interspersed with modern commercial buildings. The city hosts a marvelous arts festival and the annual Australian Grand Prix motor race. It regards itself as the wine capital of Australia, within an easy drive to the famous Barossa Valley.

Adelaide divers are fortunate because they are equidistant from most of the good diving locations. In many instances, a half hour's drive is all that is required, although some of the better diving in the state is on the Yorke Peninsula. The closest diving is on the reef system just off the beach suburb of Glenelg, and on the wreck of the *Norma* off Semaphore, near Port Adelaide.

The west coastline of the Fleurieu Peninsula south of Adelaide is a popular region. Shore diving is excellent from famous *Port Noarlunga*

There was a time when the diver could walk right out to Port Noarlunga Reef on the half-mile-long jetty, but a heavy storm tore away the last few yards — the ladder is no longer there. The mile-long reef is arguably one of the most diver-populated reefs in Australian waters due to its accessibility, only 18 miles south of Adelaide. It was declared a marine reserve in 1971.

Many varieties of leatherjackets are common in Australian temperate waters, none more attractive than the horseshoe leatherjacket (Meuschenia hippocrepis) *with its distinctive markings.*

Reef, which is one of the most popular dive sites in Australia, due predominantly to its easy access. The reef is 400 yards offshore and a mile long. An algal/mussel community dominates the reef top, whilst kelp takes over on the outer reef slope. There is a rich sponge and hydroid community at the southern end of the reef. Most of the southern, temperate-water, reef fish species may be seen here. Marine life is gradually returning since the reef was declared a marine reserve in 1971.

Aldinga Reef Aquatic Reserve is 30 miles south of Adelaide on the eastern seaboard of the Gulf of St. Vincent between Port Willunga and Aldinga Beach. The *Aldinga Drop-off* is pocketed with caves and fissures, and is rich in marine life. Gorgonia, blue devilfish, boarfish, green grouper, and many other species provide excellent opportunities for underwater photography.

The wreck of the 1,227-ton sailing ship *Star of Greece* lies in shallow water between Port Willunga and Aldinga beach. Her remains are located in 20 ft, 200 yards from shore. The wreck has been completely flattened, but iron frames, hull plating, parts of the masts, and some scattered artifacts are of historic significance; and the wreck offers fine snorkeling.

The 500-yard-long jetty at *Rapid Bay,* with its tall metal pylons, makes an excellent dive, particularly for macro photography and creative wide-angle work. The grain trade left a number of superb jetties in the Gulf of St. Vincent, which is one of the reasons for popularity of shore diving in South Australia.

Ten miles further south by road, *Cape Jervis,* at the entrance to Backstairs Passage, has a good boat ramp and is a departure point for *Kangaroo Island* and *The Pages. Fisheries Beach* is three miles southeast from Cape Jervis and can be dived from the shore.

67

Huge jetties in Spencer Gulf and St. Vincent Gulf were constructed in the 1800s to facilitate loading of grain and other produce from inland South Australia. These have long been abandoned to fishermen and grateful divers. The wooden or steel pylons attract all forms of invertebrate and fish life. This one is at Port Hughes at the north end of Spencer Gulf.

On the opposite side of the Gulf of St. Vincent, nearly fifty wrecks lie off the southern point of Yorke Peninsula. Edithburgh is very popular, with superb local diving, and is the departure point for many offshore sites. The region is famous for its magnificent seahorses. Stenhouse Bay has superb diving.

Troubridge Shoals off Edithburgh is home to giant spider crabs that claw their way over a sponge-covered reef. Troubridge Island is shallow and sandy and hence not a popular dive.

The wreck of the unique 3,596-ton single-screw, turret deck steamer *Clan Ranald* lies half a mile offshore, just west of Troubridge Hill. She is in reasonable condition, 330 ft long, and lies upside down in 80 ft on a sandy bottom. Her fittings and machinery can be seen scattered over the seabed. The ship is one of the best wreck dives to be found off the South Australian coast and particularly significant, historically, because of her construction.

With a boat, many more offshore reefs as well as the fabulous *Althorpe Islands* south of Cape Spencer at the entrance to Investigator Strait may be reached. The fish life here is second to none in the state, with huge kingfish being common. And on an exceptionally good day even *Wedge Island* can be reached from Pondalowie Bay, if you have a fast, sturdy boat.

Pondalowie Bay, on the southwestern tip of the peninsula, is a popular dive. Located 164 miles by road from Adelaide, the quiet bay has some of the finest diving in the state. Grouper up to fifty pounds are not uncommon from these areas, with some of the best diving being in the *Crystal Bay–Reef Heads* region. Big drop-offs make great territory for both scuba diving and underwater photography. Campgrounds exist at Pondalowie Bay and Marion Bay and stores at Stenhouse Bay and Marion Bay, but otherwise there are limited facilities. Be prepared to rough it. The only reasonable town, boasting a few shops and a pub, is Warooka, 35 miles from Stenhouse Bay.

It takes about three hours to drive from Adelaide to Port Victoria on the western Yorke Peninsula. From here, nearby Wardang Island may be reached by launching a boat from the ramp on the foreshore near the Port Victoria Nautical Museum. Wardang Island lies in Spencer Gulf 8 miles due west of Port Victoria, and is 6 miles by 3 miles in size. The island is managed by an aboriginal community.

All wrecks are in shallow water and have been reduced to scattered, weed-encrusted wreckage by the strength of the sea and early salvage divers looking for nonferrous metals. Only the three-masted ship *Songvaar* (1912), the French barque *Notre Dame d'Arvor* (1920), and the steamship *Australian* (1912) are worth diving. The *Songvaar* lies in 70 ft and is often partially covered in sand. She is also scattered due to nature and explosives, and visibility tends to be rather poor in the area. The *Australian* has broken up but the marine life is interesting. A boiler lies covered in weeds. Scrap metal hunters have blasted the ship beyond recognition. The *Notre Dame d'Arvor* has also deteriorated badly.

Jetty Diving

Diving from the old sailing ship piers in Spencer Gulf and the Gulf of St.Vincent is interesting: you'll find prolific invertebrate life on the pylons and incredible schools of fish. The long Port Hughes jetty jutting into Spencer Gulf is excellent, with soft corals, bryozoans, sponges, ascidians, and anemones growing on each pylon, and schooling fish parading the length of the jetty. Other excellent jetties on the Yorke Peninsula are at Ardrossan, Port Vincent, Stansbury, and Port Giles (with its 25-ft ladders); Edithburgh, on St.Vincent Gulf; and Stenhouse Bay into Investigator Strait.

Eyre Peninsula

Typical depth range:	20-80 ft
Typical current conditions:	Slight
Expertise required:	Experienced only, due to remoteness
Access:	Boat

The Eyre Peninsula is dry, remote, and intriguing. The main town, Port Lincoln, has a population of more than 10,000 with a large commercial center, fine tourist facilities, and an excellent marina; the region is popular for cruising yachts. It is also the base for Australia's largest tuna fleet. Other towns on the southeast coast and west coast tend to be fishing villages with a few holiday shacks.

Most of the shore diving near to Port Lincoln is limited, mainly due to the lack of access roads. *Wanna Beach* and *Memory Cove* are within 35 miles of the town. *Whaler's Way,* 20 miles southwest of the township, is a popular tourist region. Relics from the early whaling industry, magnificent coastal scenery, and abundant wildlife can all be seen here. *Cape Wiles,* the eastern extremity, is flanked by picturesque Fishery Bay where whales were once slaughtered. With a beautiful stretch of white sand and clean, cool water, the bay makes an ideal surfing and sunbathing retreat.

Diving off the 110-ft auxiliary ketch Falie *requires the use of "rubber ducks" to ferry divers to inshore reefs.*

Port Lincoln is the main departure point for the Sir Joseph Banks Group, Thistle Island (further south), and the Gambier Islands at the entrance to Spencer Gulf. *Spilsby Island,* southernmost and largest of the Sir Joseph Banks Group, is situated 28 miles east of Port Lincoln. The island contains many secluded beaches, rocky bays, and inlets, and is operated as a grazing property for a thousand sheep. One of the main attractions is the great flocks of Cape Barren geese that can be seen all year round, the rare sea eagle, and numerous varieties of parrots. Seventeen of the eighteen islands in the group are proclaimed conservation parks with unique birdlife, seal colonies, and historic farming homesteads. Diving is superb with clear water, corals, crayfish, seals, and prolific marine life.

Wedge Island is situated 60 miles southeast of Port Lincoln in the middle of the entrance to Spencer Gulf. It is the largest of the Gambier Group, about four miles by two miles. The island has magnificent scenery. There are 500-ft cliffs at the southern end that slope gently to a golden beach nearly a mile in length along the eastern side of the island. Although heavily grazed, the wildlife is an attraction in itself. Emus, wallabies, wombats, penguins, and a great abundance of birdlife, including sea eagles and ospreys, can be seen.

Shark Cove is on the southeast side of Wedge Island. It is an excellent dive, with superb marine life and a small cave and tunnel covered in

Topgallant Island in the Investigator Group appears as no more than a round uninhabited rock, yet below the surface lies some of the finest diving in Australian waters. Topgallant has a thousand caves and passages just waiting to be explored.

Curious and unafraid, these Australian fur seals on Pearson Island take great delight in posing for the camera.

colorful sponges, zoanthids, and anemones. Long undercuts in the vertical walls bottom out at about 80 ft. Small yellow gorgonian sea fans protrude from the cliff edge whilst delicate anemones and solitary hydroids, bright yellow zoanthids, and sponges of all colors cover the protected underhangs and ledges. Leafy sea dragons may be seen in the area.

The *Investigator Group* is five main islands in the Great Australian Bight, lying 35 miles west of Cape Finnis near Elliston. *Flinders Island* is the largest, but smaller *Pearson Island* and tiny *Topgallant Isle* offer the best diving. Very few sport divers visit the group due to its remoteness.

Pearson Island is best dived from a live-aboard boat, as it is the furthest of the islands from Elliston, 36 miles southwest. The island is shaped like a figure eight with a very narrow isthmus joining its two halves. There is a wallaby colony and several large seal colonies.

The Dice on the southeast side of southern Pearson Island has huge cube-shaped boulders forming caverns and tunnels that harbor prolific marine life. The variety of invertebrates and fish epitomizes the beauty of southern temperate waters, particularly in a region that is rarely visited.

Bonney and Clyde is an incredible dive site on small Topgallant Isle, 20 miles northeast of Pearson. The rock island is riddled with holes, caves, tunnels, and swimthroughs, most of which have never been dived. This is true exploratory diving, and it is rated as one of the best dives in Australia. The main island is no more than a huge rock outcrop. Pelagic and reef fish species abound; there are seals, large blue grouper and blue devilfish, exquisite harlequin fish; and a terrain rich in marine life — red, orange, and yellow gorgonia, basket stars, sponges, and every imaginable temperate-water invertebrate.

With a macabre sense of humor, divers have named this site Bonney and Clyde — because it is riddled with holes.

The Great White Shark

Divers appear to have a morbid fascination for the great white shark, *Carcharodon carcharias*. We both fear and respect this magnificent creature and it is little wonder that many of us would like to see the animal in its natural habitat — preferably while we are safe in a boat or a dive cage. Over the past few years, Australian and overseas divers have been attracted to Port Lincoln waters because of the great whites. Led by shark expert Rodney Fox, himself a victim of a White Pointer attack off Aldinga in 1963, professional and amateur videographers film the shark in waters south of Spencer Gulf, usually near the Neptune Islands. The waters are strewn with blood and guts to bring in the animals. This has angered many divers and the practice is questionable. Similar action by a game fishing competition in 1988 resulted, some say, in the death by shark attack of a snorkeler near Port Lincoln. No matter what the moral judgment may be, the southern waters of South Australia, and in particular southern Spencer Gulf, are known as habitat for great white sharks. This should not preclude diving, however. Under normal circumstances the great white is not interested in the diver. But diving with seals could lead to a case of mistaken identity, and diving anywhere near chummed waters is asking for trouble unless you are protected in a shark cage.

One of the most colorful of the temperate-water species (and most inquisitive), the harlequin fish (Othos dentex) is distinguished by its bright blue and yellow markings over a brilliant red-orange body. It is common in South Australian waters.

6

Tasmania

Bicheno

Typical depth range:	20-100 ft
Typical current conditions:	None to moderate
Expertise required:	Novice to experienced
Access:	Boat

Tasmania is a magnificent island of contrasts: long rolling fields reminiscent of an English pastoral scene and jagged, forested mountains; tiny protected bays with white sand beaches and inaccessible coves and cliffs; tiny country villages and modern commercial cities such as the historic capital Hobart, and Launceston.

Tall trunks of kelp rise to the surface in one of the many kelp forests off Bicheno on Tasmania's east coast. Photo courtesy of Tony Douglas, Bicheno Dive Centre.

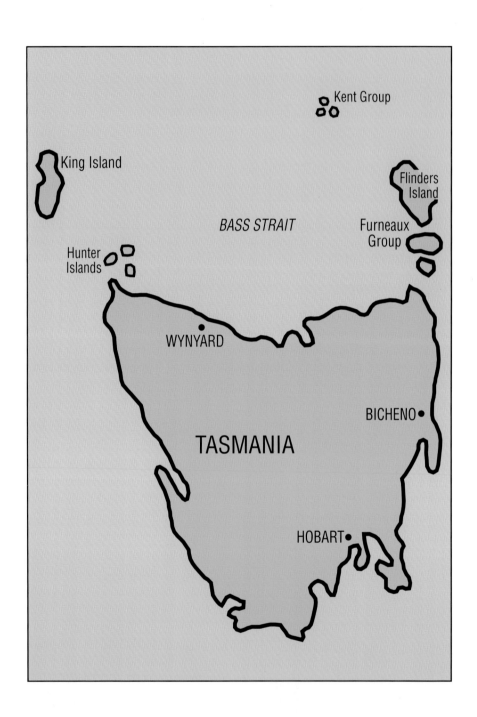

Shaped roughly like an inverted pyramid, the island is 170 miles across the northern coast, and the same north to south. The 125-mile road from Hobart to Launceston takes about three hours, and goes through beautiful countryside.

There are two main population regions; the southeast sector with Hobart at its center; and the central north coast encompassing Launceston on the Tamar River, and the coastal towns of Devonport, Burnie, and Wynyard. The central-west and southwest parts of the state are mountainous and stunningly beautiful, and the location of one of the most magnificent national parks in all of Australia. Cradle Mountain National Park extends from the midwest region, linking up with the Franklin River region at Wild Rivers National Park, and then continues on to the remote South West National Park.

Hobart and Launceston are serviced by Australian domestic airlines. There is also a vehicle ferry service between Melbourne and Devonport, and between Port Welshpool (eastern Victoria) and Georgetown at the head of the Tamar River.

Bicheno. The tiny fishing village of *Bicheno* has some of the finest temperate-water diving in the world. The town is located on the central east coast of Tasmania, 100 miles by road from Launceston and 87 miles north of Hobart. Bicheno has a fine divers' lodge and a well equipped dive charter service.

The brilliant temperate-water diving is due to miles of rocky coastline and offshore rocks and reefs covered in rich and varied marine life. Diving need rarely be below 60 ft, and most of the good dive sites are only a matter of minutes by boat from Bicheno jetty.

The *Giant Kelp Forests* attract photographers prepared to use a bit of imagination in their work. Kelp trees tower up from 100 ft and appear like a magnificent underwater forrest. *The Castle* has huge granite bommies rising from 120 ft to within 20 ft of the surface. There is a vertical drop-off on the southeast side with undercut rock faces covered in zoanthids, sponges, and bryozoans. A 50-ft-long tunnel is home to hundreds of crayfish. The site has prolific fish life, particularly boarfish.

Bird Rock is a granite monolith surrounded by huge boulders forming a number of caves and tunnels. The area is teeming with fish. *Muirs Rock* has a large submarine complex with numerous caves and tunnels from 6 ft down to 60 ft. *Trap Reef* rises out of 100 ft to within 20 ft and is known for its schools of butterfly perch and large sponge gardens.

North Coast. Excellent diving exists all along the north, northeast, and northwest coastlines of Tasmania. *Cape Naturaliste* on the northeastern tip is a particularly attractive area, but beware of the weather as it can blow up with little notice. *Rocky Cape,* to the west of Wynyard, is excellent for crays. Check the weather as the area is subject to prevailing westerly winds and can become very rough. A large dive complex operates out of Wynyard.

Huge kelp fronds cover the seabed on many southern coastal reefs, some rising 60 ft to the surface.

South Coast. *Hobart* is a delightful city; historical and modern buildings nestle under the shadow of Mt. Wellington on a magnificent harbor. Many of Hobart's beautiful early colonial sandstone buidings were erected by the sweat and toil of the unfortunate convicts who formed the majority of the settlement in 1804. A trip past Eaglehawk Neck down the Tasman Penninsula to the convict ruins at Port Arthur just barely recalls the horrors of one of Australia's penal colonies.

Tasmania's notorious penal settlement at Port Arthur now attracts more than 200,000 tourists a year, few of whom appreciate the degradation and hardships of the twelve thousand convicts who passed through, or passed on, from the settlement.

Although more prolific in northern waters, the fascinating feather star or crinoid can be found in warmer temperate waters, its delicate pinnules (arms) waving in the current to trap nutrients. Southern species tend to be rather shy and hence rarely seen, hiding in crevices.

Deep Glen Bay situated on the Forestier Peninsula north of Eaglehawk Neck is known for its superb caves and a wide variety of marine life. Further south, the Tasman Peninsula is a popular dive location. *Tasman Arch*, the *Devil's Kitchen* and *Blowhole*, *Waterfall Bay* with its superb caves, and the *Isle of the Dead*, with massive kelp forests are all excellent dives. Depths vary from 20 ft to 60 ft with visibility often exceeding 100 ft in winter. Southern right whales are seen frequently south of the peninsula.

On the southeast coast of the Tasman Peninsula, Fortesque Bay is surrounded by yet another national park. There is excellent shallow water diving here, very clear and usually well protected.

Eleven wrecks have been scuttled in Storm Bay at the *Wreck Graveyard* near Betsy Island, just fifteen minutes by boat from South Arm.

Bruny Island provides some protection for the D'Entrecasteaux Channel which has excellent diving down to 120 ft. The midchannel area is popular with divers, particularly *Huon Island, Arch Island, Simpsons Point,* and *Nine Pin Point. Acteon Island, Recherche Bay,* and *South East Cape* are all excellent but be wary of the weather in these exposed locations.

Extensive kelp forests occur in the area from *Dover* on *Port Esperance* down to Southport. It is not far from Dover that the most popular of Tasmanian wrecks can be found. The 440-ton barque *Katherine Shearer* is only ten minutes by boat from the Dover ramp. She went down in 1855.

The rugged southwest cape of Tasmania is virgin territory for divers. The remote *Maatsuyker Islands* are rarely visited and the entrance to Port Davey is challenging — just to get there is an effort and needs careful planning. Two thousand miles south lies King George V Land in Antarctica.

Bass Strait Islands

Typical depth range:	20-100 ft
Typical current conditions:	Minor to moderate
Expertise required:	Experienced, due to remoteness
Access:	Boat and shore

Bass Strait has been compared to the infamous Bermuda Triangle directly opposed on the other side of the world. Ships and aircraft have disappeared without traces but the mystery is diminished when one understands the treacherous seas of this narrow channel between Tasmania and mainland Australia.

At the western entrance lies King Island; the eastern entrance has the Kent Group, and Flinders Island in the Furneaux Group. The Kent Group can only be reached by boat. There are air services from Tasmania and Victoria to Flinders Island and King Island. Only Flinders Island and King Island have accommodations and dive operators. Most other islands are uninhabited. Other than Flinders Island, most islands in the eastern region require permission before landing as they are either Government-controlled or privately owned.

Kent Group. The eastern Bass Strait islands of the Kent Group lie 55 miles south-southeast from Wilson's Promontory (Victoria). There are four main islands. The largest of the group is *Deal Island*, less than four miles long and rising a thousand feet at its southern end near the lighthouse.

Beautiful West Cove on remote Erith Island is visited only by the occasional "yachtie" and diver. Deal Island lies in the distance, across Murray Pass. The wreck of the Bulli *lies in 60 ft around the point on the left.*

Three-hundred-foot-high cliffs plunge straight down to the depths, providing incredible wall diving off Deal Island in the Kent Group, in eastern Bass Strait. Ledges and crevices are home for thousands of crayfish.

Diving the islands is superb. South of Deal Island, in particular, there are sheer vertical cliffs that continue straight down into the depths. On the northeast are shallow seagrass covered areas with small caves hiding crayfish. With so few people traveling over to "The Group," most sites are unexplored. The wreck of the 540-ton steamship *Bulli* lies in 60 ft of water in West Cove (Erith Island) and is an excellent dive. The wreck of the 1,376-ton steamship *Karitane* in Squally Cove is good diving although she is well flattened. Several other wrecks have yet to be found.

Furneaux Group. The Furneaux Group, of which *Flinders Island* is the largest, lies at the eastern end of Bass Strait and stretches for 70 miles north to south. Fifty islands make up the group, with settlements on Flinders Island and Cape Barren Island.

Flinders Island is 40 by 18 miles, with a magnificent mountain range capped by Strezlecki Peak at 2,400 ft. The western shores have excellent beaches as do the northeast shores of the island. The eastern shores also have long white beaches but they are relatively inaccessible, with marshland and poor tracks.

The Furneaux Group offers superb diving, for both wrecks and marine life. The best way to dive the islands is by charter boat, or to stay at Lady Barron and go on organized day trips. There is good shore diving off Flinders Island, but a boat is preferred to reach the smaller islands.

With an obviously characteristic shape, the fishbone sea fan (Mopsea encrinula) *adds pink, white, and yellow to the seabed. This species is quite common in southern waters.*

to Grassy on the east coast, drops down from 36 to 95 ft and is covered with zoanthids and sponges, plenty of crays, and schooling fish. The *Blowhole* is shallow-water diving, less than 30 ft, with sandstone ledges and caves. Boarfish, morwong, trumpeter, and sweep are always found, as well as crayfish and abalone.

Due to exceptionally clear waters coming directly in from Bass Strait, *Grassy Harbour* is a fine dive with fields of bull kelp and rocky outcrops. The harbor wall has a 40 ft drop with crays, abalone, and many fish. *The Cliffs at Seal Rocks* drop down to 100 ft with superb marine life, schools of fish, crayfish, and dramatic underwater scenery.

The crayfish industry in southern Australia is centered on the rock lobster Jasus novaehollandiae, *which is also known to excite many divers who find this common crustacean in caves and beneath ledges. The southern rock lobster has no pincer claws, and can grow to up to two feet.*

Appendix: Dive Services and Organizations

This list is included as a service to the reader. The author has made every effort to make the list complete at the time this book was printed. This list does not constitute an endorsement of these operators and dive shops. The Telecom Yellow Pages Directory is a useful guide to services in capital cities. Services indicated with an asterisk have diver lodge accommodation. If operators/owners wish to be included in future reprints/editions, please contact Pisces Books, P.O. Box 2608, Houston, Texas 77252-2608.

SERVICES

Byron Bay

Byron Bay Dive Centre *
9 Lawson St., Byron Bay, NSW 2481
Ph: 066-856587 Fax: 066-857942

Sundive Dive Centre
Lawson and Fletcher Sts.
Byron Bay, NSW 2481
Ph: 066-857755 Fax: 066-858361

Solitary Islands

Dive Quest
30 Mullaway Dr.
Mullaway, NSW 2456
Ph: 066-541930

Coffs Harbour Dive Centre
396 High St.
Coffs Harbour, NSW 2450
Ph: 066-522422 Fax: 066-525702

North Coast
New South Wales

South West Rocks Dive Centre
100 Gregory St.
South West Rocks, NSW 2431
Ph: 065-666474 Fax: 065-666474

Port Macquarie Dive Centre
Shop 7, Port Marina
Port Macquarie, NSW 2444
Ph: 065-838483 Fax: 065-835777

Action Divers Tuncurry
Shop 4, 17 Manning St.
Tuncurry, NSW 2428
Ph: 065-554053

Forster Dive Centre
15 Little St., Forster, NSW 2428
Ph: 065 545255

Action Divers
Shop 14, Nelson Towers
73A Victoria Parade
Nelson Bay, NSW 2315
Ph: 049-812491

The Dive Shop
708 Hunter St.
Newcastle, NSW 2304
Ph: 048-294234

Action Divers Belmont
430 Pacific Highway
Belmont, NSW 2280
Ph: 049-453676

Norah Head Dive Shop
16 Michell St.
Norah Head, NSW 2263
Ph: 043-963652

Pro Dive Central Coast
411 The Entrance
Long Jetty, NSW 2261
Ph: 043-341559

Dolphin Dive
77 Beaumont Av.
Wyoming, NSW 2250
Ph: 048-244596

Greater Sydney

Aqua Sports Pty. Ltd.
430 Hume Highway
Yagoona, Sydney, NSW 2199
Ph: 02-7082826

Dive 2000
2 Military Rd.
Neutral Bay, Sydney, NSW 2089
Ph: 02-9537783 Fax: 02-9532245

Deep Six Diving
1057 Victoria Rd.
West Ryde, Sydney, NSW 2114
Ph: 02-8584299

Frog Dive Kingsford
479 Anzac Parade
Kingsford, NSW 2032

Frog Dive Merrylands
7A Miller St., Merrylands, NSW 2160
Ph: 02-6372144

Frog Dive Willoughby
539 Willoughby Rd.
Willoughby, NSW 2068
Ph: 02-9585699

Fun Dive
255-257 Stanmore Rd.
Petersham, Sydney, NSW 2049
Ph: 02-5695284

Fathom Diving
174 Sydney Rd., Fairlight, NSW 2094
Ph: 02-9496255

Pro Dive Drummoyne
227 Victoria Rd.
Drummoyne, Sydney, NSW 2047
Ph: 02-8197639

Pro Dive Mid City
478 George St., Sydney, NSW 2000
Ph: 02-2646177

Penrith Dive Centre
1/20 Castlereagh St.
Penrith, NSW 2750
Ph: 047-323511

Pro Dive Penrith
97C Henry St., Penrith, NSW 2750
Ph: 047-312866

Sub-Aquatic Training
484 King Georges Rd.
Beverley Hills, NSW 2209
Ph: 02-5704222

St.George Underwater Centre
458 King Georges Rd.
Beverley Hills, NSW 2209
Ph: 02-500268 Fax: 02-5024657

Shiprock Dive
617 Port Hacking Rd.
Lilli Pilli, NSW 2229
Ph: 02-5262664 Fax: 02-5262906

South of Sydney

United Divers
6 Victoria St.
Wollongong, NSW 2500
Ph: 042-285962

Illawarra Aqua Centre
235 Windang Rd.
Windang, NSW 2503
Ph: 042-964215 Fax: 042-964215

Coastwide Diving Services
41 Addison St.
Shellharbour, NSW 2529
Ph: 042-964266

Jervis Bay

Aqua-Shack Divers Lodge *
Hawke and Nowra Sts.
Huskisson, NSW 2540
Ph: 044-416363

Jervis Bay Seasports*
47 Owen St., Huskisson, NSW 2540
Ph: 044-415012 Fax: 044-416723

Pro-Dive Jervis Bay
Shop 6, 74 Owen St.
Huskisson, NSW 2540
Ph: 044-415215

Southern New South Wales

Merimbula Divers Lodge *
28 Park St., Merimbula, NSW 2548
Ph: 064-953611 Fax: 064-953648

Sea Trek School of the Sea
7 Beach St., Thathra, NSW 2550
and 37 Princes Highway
Merimbula, NSW 2548
Ph: 064-941985

The Ocean Hut
Town Centre
Narooma, NSW 2546
Ph: 044-762278

Wilsons Promontory

Deep Down Diver Education
RMB 7411, Sale, Victoria 3851
Ph: 051-498296

Linda-Jade Dive Charters
Bowen St., Port Franklin, Vic. 3964
Ph: 056-862466

Tasy's Dive Shop
Cashin St., Inverloch, Vic. 3996
Ph: 056-741848

Vera-Jan Charters
Tarraville Rd., Port Albert, Vic. 3971
Ph: 051-832347

Port Phillip Bay

Melbourne Dive Services

Associated Divers
1292 Centre Rd.
Clayton, Melbourne 3168
Ph: 03-5449002

Bob Cumberland's Dive Shop
Hampshire and Blackburn Rds.
Glen Waverley, Melbourne 3150
Ph: 03-5612096

Dive Experience
82 Fergusson St.
Williamstown, Vic. 3016
Ph: 03-3975139

Diving Headquarters
436 High St.
Prahran, Melbourne 3181
Ph: 03-519081

In Depth Scuba Education *
580 Victoria St.
North Melbourne, Vic. 3051
Ph: 03-3283218
Melbourne Diving Services
144 Bell St.
West Heidelberg, Melbourne 3081
Ph: 03-4594111 Fax: 03-4599942

Ocean Divers
237 East Boundary Rd.
East Bentleigh, Melbourne 3156
Ph: 03-5792851

Outer Melbourne Services

Adventure Down Under
604 Mountain Highway
Bayswater, Vic. 3153
Ph: 03-7295811

Diveline
6 Young St., Frankston, Vic. 3199
Ph: 03-7837405

Interdive
242 Burwood Highway
Upper Ferntree Gully, Vic. 3156
Ph: 03-7588333 Fax: 03-7522801

Paradise Divers
114 Carlton Rd.
Dandenong, Vic. 3175
Ph: 03-7935248

Southern Port Phillip Bay

D.I.S. Divers Lodge *
46 Canterbury Jetty Rd.
Blairgowrie, Vic. 3942
Ph: 059-889711

Diver Instruction Services
(and dive charters)
Nepean Highway, Portsea, Vic. 3944
Ph: 059-845155

Geelong Dive Centre
178 Moorabool St.
Geelong Vic. 3220
Ph: 052-213342

Guidelines for Temperate Water Diving

1. Divers trained for or familiar with tropical water diving must be aware of the different physical conditions that will be experienced with temperate water diving. If unfamiliar with temperate water diving, inform the divemaster accordingly.
2. When determining weights required, consider wetsuit compression with depth of dive, resulting in increased negative buoyancy. Do not overweight.The thicker the wetsuit, the greater the number of weights required to neutralize the buoyancy of the suit. Ensure that the weight-belt fits firmly and that you are familiar with the quick-release mechanism.
3. Ensure that the wetsuit fits comfortably, and is of a suitable material and thickness to prevent hypothermia.
4. Be familiar with temperate water animals, many of which have characteristics dissimilar with tropical animals.
5. Temperate seas may exhibit strong currents and change suddenly, particularly in summer. Calm seas can be deceptive. Always determine current intensity and direction before entering water.
6. Always wear a knife, a decided advantage should the diver be entangled in kelp.
7. Be aware of the legal implications of the dive, particularly when diving on a shipwreck, near jetties, in marine parks, in shipping channels, and when taking marine animals for food or collection.
8. Do not harass marine mammals such as whales and dolphins. Laws prohibit diving with whales in certain locations.
9. Be aware of the implications of diving within a seal colony. Do not approach close to seals on land.
10. If diving from a boat, be aware of boat etiquette and safety requirements.
11. Always seek local knowledge before diving.
12. Never enter caves or tunnels, nor penetrate a shipwreck, without local knowledge. Sudden changes in sea conditions can result in dangerous surge.
13. Diver fitness plays a greater role in temperate water, due to the possibility of stronger currents, thick wetsuit encumbrance, and unfamiliarity (hence anxiety). Be aware of your capabilities.
14. If diving without the services of a dive charter operator or guide familiar with the area, be aware of emergency services available. Prepare a contingency plan "just in case." Commit the Diving Emergency Service number to memory.
15. It is sound advice not to take a camera on the first dive in unfamiliar territory.
16. Do not touch delicate marine animals. Adopt the general principle of "look but don't touch." Avoid excessive finning near marine growth. Ensure that all gauges and combo units do not hang free.

Diving Emergency Service

The Diving Emergency Service is a central contact point that may be called from anywhere in Australia, including ship radio. DES will make emergency arrangements including transport to a decompression chamber, if required. Medical assistance is available at this number so that appropriate first aid advice is provided.

(008) 008 200
State: "This is a diving emergency."
Give: Details of the incident —
  • The exact location of patient, patient's name, and age.
  • Telephone number where someone can be contacted, including STD code. This should be given immediately just in case the phone is cut off. Make sure that someone is on standby at the phone and that the phone is not used for any other purpose.
  • Details of the accident or incident and the patient's condition.
  • Current first aid being applied.
  • Your name or name of contact.
  • Have any other emergency, medical, or police services been notified and if so, who and when.

Check: That the following have been correctly recorded by having the operator repeat them back to you.

1. Location
2. Telephone number
3. Dive details
4. Symptoms
5. Contact name

State Hyperbaric Unit Contacts

Victoria (03) 520 2811
Prince Alfred Hospital, Commercial Road, Prahran

South Australia (08) 244 5514
Royal Adelaide Hospital

Tasmania (002) 30 0110
Royal Hobart Hospital

New South Wales (02) 960 0321
RAN School of Underwater Medicine, HMAS Penguin, Balmoral

Index